ROME · FLORENCE

THE VATICAN-TIVOLI   **FIESOLE-SAN MINIATO AL MONTE**

VENICE · NAPLES

MURANO-TORCELLO   **POMPEII-HERCULANEUM-SORRENTO**
CAPRI-ISCHIA-AMALFI-PAESTUM

500 COLOR PHOTOGRAPHS · CITY MAPS

BET
BONECHI EDIZIONI "IL TURISMO"

Reprint 2006

© Copyright by Bonechi Edizioni "Il Turismo" S.r.l.
Via G. Di Vittorio, 31 - 50145 FIRENZE
Tel. +39-055 37.57.39 / 34.24.527
Fax +39-055 37.47.01
E-mail: bbonechi@dada.it
        info@bonechionline.com
http: //www.bonechionline.com
Printed in Italy
All rights reserved

Publishing editor: Barbara Bonechi
Text revision and iconographic research: Lorena Lazzari
Text on page 173 of "The city underground" is by Giuliano Valdes.
Graphic design and layout: Sabrina Menicacci
Cover and photo retouching: Paola Rufino
English translations: Studio Comunicare
Photographs: Archives of Bonechi Edizioni "Il Turismo", Giuseppe Carfagna (Rome),
Casa Editrice V. Carcavallo (Naples), Nicola Grifoni (Florence), Marco Iarossi (Florence),
Nicola Quartullo (Rome), Rabatti & Domingie (Florence), V.I.P. (Naples).
The photos of the Sansevero Chapel in Naples are by V.I.P. (Naples).
The photo on page 73 (center) was kindly granted by Cassa di Risparmio di Firenze.
The plan of Naples was kindly granted by the Casa Editrice V. Carcavallo (Naples).
Photolithography: Fotolito Immagine, Florence
Printed by: Lito Terrazzi, Firenze

ISBN 88-7204-528-2

Dear Reader,

My hopes, in this book, are to introduce you
to some of the loveliest cities in Italy, defined by some
as the "garden" of the world. The brief but interesting
information that accompanies the pictures
will lead you along an "itinerary" with a wealth of monuments,
museums, palaces and churches.
Rome, Florence, Venice and Naples, four cities quite unlike
each other yet sharing a radiant splendor, and furnishing
an overview and synthesis of a marvelous civilization
that has begun its journey in the third millennium.

Bon voyage, dear reader!   *The Publisher*

Rome "Caput Mundi"

The eternal city, caput mundi *(capital of the world)*, Urbs *(City)* – these are some of the names used to describe Rome, capital and largest city of Italy, and with a wealth of historical, artistic and spiritual values that set it apart from any other city in the world. While Rome and Athens were both the cradle of Western civilization, the difference between the two is enormous. The visible remains of Rome's past are not confined to a single "historical section", but rather spread throughout her entire metropolitan fabric in a vital overlapping of periods and

styles. The city that was the capital of the greatest empire of antiquity is now, as it has been for centuries, also the capital of Christianity, and the spiritual center of the Roman Catholic world. In its enviable location on the Tiber River, twenty miles from the Mediterranean, modern-day Rome sprawls over its hills and fuses the monumentality of the historical center (with its ancient ruins, great basilicas, Renaissance palaces, baroque piazzas) with the vast disorderly suburbs and intense and often

chaotic traffic of a modern metropolis. The historical center itself has many facets, ranging from the great modern thoroughfares that connect its vital centers (for example, Via Nazionale, Corso Vittorio Emanuele II), the elegant famous streets with fashionable shops and cafes (Via Veneto, Via Condotti) or art galleries and antique shops (Via Margutta, Via del Babuino), the popular districts (such as the celebrated picturesque Trastevere quarter). Rome is also a lively cultural center, boasting countless museums, libraries, international universities and research centers, peerless archives, theaters and concert halls, with of note the Teatro dell'Opera and the Accademia Musicale di Santa Cecilia. The prestigious Roman University La Sapienza is one of the largest in Europe and is flanked by other universities and important pontifical academies. But the principal aspects of Roman life are elsewhere: as a political capital of a modern state with over 60 million inhabitants (and therefore hosting the offices of the President of the Republic, of the Government, of the two Houses of Parliament, of the Ministries and the highest authorities of the Republic). Rome is also the headquarters of the Papal See and the College of Cardinals and the Roman curia flank the head of the Church. The city is moreover one of the major centers in the world for tourism as well as one of the most important pilgrimage centers (especially during religious festivities or when a Holy Year is proclaimed by the Pontiff.

ROMA

The Roman Forum

S ituated at the junction of the Palatine, Capitoline, and Esquiline hills, the Roman Forum was for centuries the site of the city's most important public buildings. The major monuments include the **Arch of Septimius Severus**, erected in 203 A.D., a superb honorary triple arch with bas-reliefs celebrating Rome's victories over the Parthians, Arabs and Adiabenians. Nearby are the **Rostra**, or public speaking platform, so called because once decorated with the rostrums (beaks) of captured war-galleys, the **Curia**, or brick Senate building, and the **Basilica Aemilia**, an immense Republican period building that rose alongside the Senate of which only little remains. On the Capitoline side are the **Temple of Saturn** (eight Ionic columns in granite and entablature) built in 497 B.C., the **Temple of Vespasian** with three corner Corinthian columns, and the **Portico of the Dei Consentes** (in honor of Olympus' twelve major deities) built in the 4th century A.D. and thus probably the last pagan monument in Rome. On the Palatine side are the

▲ Arch of Septimius Severus

▼ Remains of the Basilica Aemilia

◄ Curia

▶ Temple of Antoninus and Faustina

▲ Temple of Castor and Pollux and Temple of Vesta

▶ Statue
of a Vestal
Virgin

Temple of Castor and Pollux with three Corinthian columns, built in 484 B.C. to honor the warlike Heavenly Twins or *Dioscuri*; the **Temple of Vesta**, a circular colonnade of Corinthian columns, and the atrium and a few statues of the **House of the Vestal Virgins** (the Vestal priestesses were responsible for seeing that the sacred fire dedicated to the goddess Vesta never went out); the **Temple of Antoninus and Faustina** built in the 2nd century A.D. by the Senate in honor of Emperor Antoninus Pius and his wife Faustina (the building's original pronaos of six Corinthian columns has survived as the porch of the church of **San Lorenzo in Miranda**); the **Basilica of Maxentius**, an immense building begun by Maxentius and completed by Constantine (of the 35-meter-tall aisled building, two of the four huge nave piers have survived); and the **Arch of Titus** at the highest

▶ The garden in the house
of the Vestal Virgins

point of the **Via Sacra** that crossed the whole Forum, a one-arched triumphal gateway built to commemorate Titus' late 1st century A.D. defeat of the Jews. While many of the monuments in the Forum are only shadows of what they were, they still provide the visitor with the emotion of a journey back through time.

▼▶ Arch of Titus and Basilica of Maxentius

Imperial Forums

▶▲ Trajan's Column
and a detail of the marvelous frieze

The first of the Imperial Forums, Caesar's, was built in 54 B.C. when the Roman Forum proved too small for the capital's ever-growing public activities. Trajan's, chronologically the last to be built, ranks as the largest. An entire medieval district was torn down to make way for the **Via dei Fori Imperiali** built in 1933 to traverse Rome's greatest archeological zone and below which much is still waiting to be discovered. Starting from Piazza Venezia, the first forum you encounter is **Trajan's Forum** built under the supervision of Apollodorus of Damascus, the renowned architect in the emperor's service from 107 to 114 A.D. *Trajan's Column* was built in 113 A.D., probably by Apollodorus himself, to commemorate the emperor's victory over the Dacians. Thirty-five meters tall, it is adorned with a continuous relief with 2500 figures that spirals approximately 200 meters around the column recounting *episodes from the Dacian war*. The *statue of St. Peter* on top was added in the 17th century to replace that of Trajan. **Trajan's Market**, set in a hemicycle against the Quirinal hill, provide a lively picture of life in the period, with rows of shops on two levels and a large covered hall, with other shops, on the third. Facing the marketplace was **Caesar's Forum**, surrounded on three sides by a portico with the entrances of other shops (*tabernae*) underneath. A section of entablature sustained by three Corinthian columns is all that remains of the **Temple of Venus Genitrix**, commissioned by Caesar in fulfillment of a vow made before the Battle of Pharsalus fought in 48 B.C. **Augustus' Forum**, situated alongside the marketplace, was girthed by a massive stone wall serving

▲ The Columns of the Basilica Ulpia (Trajan's Forum)

▲ Trajan's Market

to isolate it from the frequent fires which broke out in the neighboring working-class district of Suburra. The **Temple of Mars Ultor** (of which the base, some columns, and sections of cella wall are extant) was built to commemorate the Roman victory in the Battle of Philippi. In **Nerva's Forum** the so-called *Colonnacce* support a lovely fragment of a frieze with a relief of women engaged in domestic pursuits, of which Minerva, to whom the temple was dedicated, was the patron.

▲ Trajan's Market

▼ Caesar's Forum

▲ The Statue of Augustus in Via dei Fori Imperiali

◄ Forum of Augustus

Colosseum

The **Flavian Amphitheater,** better known as the Colosseum, has been the symbol of the greatness and power of Rome for centuries. It is also probably one of the most famous buildings of antiquity and in the world. The enormous project was begun by Vespasian in 72 A.D. and inaugurated by Titus eight years later. It has been attributed to Rabirius, the architect of Domitian's Palace. The amphitheater, the largest monument of the Roman civilization, is elliptical in shape, measures 188 x 156 meters, and is 57 meters tall. The four-story structure is wholly faced in travertine. The exterior consisted of three floors of eighty round arches in the Classical progression (Doric topped by Ionic topped by Corinthian) and an upper floor composed of a wall divided by

▼ The Colosseum and detail of a relief with gladiators fighting wild animals (Vatican Museums)

were open to all Roman citizens, distributed according to social class, and comprised tournaments, exhibitions and spectacular mock sea battles. No documentary evidence exists to back up the story of the martyrdom of Christians. Gladiator fights, although still popular, were outlawed by Honorius in 404, while animal combats continued into the 6th century. Throughout the Middle Ages, the Colosseum was used as a handy quarry for building material. In addition, all the metal clamps between the facing blocks were removed over the centuries, leaving the holes still visible today. The **subterranean chambers** where the animals were once caged under the arena before the games can be viewed inside.

▲ Access beneath the cavea

pilaster strips with alternating windows. The opening was memorable with festivities lasing for 100 days while other grandiose celebrations marked the 1000th anniversary of the founding of Rome in 249 A.D. The frequent celebrations

▼ Interior of the Colosseum

▲ Arch of Constantine with
the Colosseum in the background

Arch of Constantine

▼ Detail of the marble reliefs
on the Arch of Constantine

One of the best preserved of the Roman triumphal arches, this celebrated monument embodies Rome's final artistic flowering which took place in the early 4th century A.D. It was built in 315 to commemorate Constantine's victory over Maxentius in the battle of Pons Milvius in 312. The 21-meter-tall, 25-meter-long triple arch contains statues and reliefs from pre-existing buildings, framed by immense Corinthian columns: the eight *statues* of Dacians above the columns originally adorned Trajan's Forum, the *medallions* with hunting and sacrificial scenes date from the first half of the 2nd century A.D., while the uppermost *reliefs* of battle scenes and imperial triumphs belonged to a building commemorating Marcus Aurelius. Nearby was the **Meta Sudans**, a cone-shaped fountain of the 1st century A.D. from which water oozed.

The Palatine

The hill believed by the Romans to be the site of Romulus' mythical founding of the city is actually where the earliest settlements (9th-8th centuries B.C.) rose. Later it became an exclusive residential district with a sumptuous imperial palace and numerous patrician villas. During the 16th century most of it was transformed into the Farnese family estate. Remains of Domitian's **Imperial Palace**, built in the late 1st century A.D., include the **Hippodrome** (160 meters long); the **Domus Flavia**, and **Domus Augustana**, the majestic palace overlooking the Circus Maximus and built as Emperor's private residence. Other sights on the Palatine, a particularly evocative sight

▲ Old street that leads to the Palatine Hill

▼ Hippodrome of Domitian

with its dense vegetation, include the **Temple of Cybele**, built in 204 B.C. in honor of the *Magna Mater* (Earth Mother goddess) and the **House of Livia** (Augustus' wife), in which several frescoes have survived.

Santa Maria d'Aracoeli

▲ Octagonal labyrinth fountain and large oval fountain (Palace of Domitian)

The church rises on the spot where the Sibyl supposedly foretold the coming of the Son of God to the Emperor Augustus in words that referred to the celestial altar, from whence the name. A steep flight of stairs leads up to the plain 14th century facade. Inside are some beautiful columns, reused, and fine frescoes by Pinturicchio.

▼ The interior of Santa Maria d'Aracoeli

▶ The fourteenth century facade of Santa Maria d'Aracoeli

Capitoline Hill

On the Campidoglio (or Capitoline Hill), the acropolis of ancient Rome, rose the temples of the greatly venerated Capitoline Jupiter and Juno Moneta facing in the direction of the Roman Forum. It has always remained the political center of the city and still hosts Rome's City Hall. The hill was remodeled by Michelangelo in the 16th century. The great ramp leads up to the remarkable **Piazza del Campidoglio**, surrounded by three great buildings. At the far end is

▲ The Capitoline staircase with the statues of the *Dioscuri*

▼ The Palace of the Senate in Piazza del Campidoglio

▶The *Equestrian statue of Marcus Aurelius*

▼ *Capitoline Venus*, Roman copy of a Hellenistic statue

the **Palace of the Senate**, which rises on the site of the *Tabularium* (Roman state archives). Apart from its fine external staircase (designed by Michelangelo), the palace was built between 1582 and 1605 by Giacomo Della Porta and Girolamo Ri-

naldi. The twin buildings leading up to it, **Palazzo dei Conservatori** on the right and **Palazzo Nuovo** on the left, were both designed by Michelangelo and built by the same architects. Today they house the Capitoline Museums. In the center of the square is Michelangelo's base for the celebrated 2nd century A.D. gilded bronze *equestrian statue of Marcus Aurelius* (the original is in the Capitoline Museums).

The Capitoline Museums

Pope Sixtus IV bequeathed the first nucleus of the collection in 1471 (which makes this the oldest public collection in existence). It has been divided into three separate museums. The *Museo dei Conservatori* contains one of the world's finest collections of Greek and Roman sculpture. Its highlights include: *Apollo with a Bow,*

a 5th century Greek original; a colossal statue of *Athena,* a copy of a 430 B.C. original by Cresilas; the so-called 1st century B.C. *Esquiline Venus*; a colossal *head of Constantine,* in bronze (marble fragments of another *colossal statue of Constantine* are in the courtyard). The collection in the *Pinacoteca Capitolina* focuses mainly on 16th-18th

▶ *Capitoline Wolf*, 6th-5th cent. B.C.

◄Sarcophagus with scenes
of battle between
Greeks and Galatians

▲ *Bust of a Lady*, 1ˢᵗ cent. A.D.

◄ *Boy removing a thorn*,
1ˢᵗ century B.C. bronze

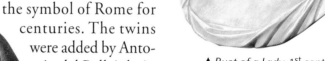

century painting. Among the most noteworthy: Titian's *Baptism of Christ*, Lorenzo Lotto's *Portrait of a Soldier*, Rubens' *Romulus and Remus Nursed by the She-Wolf*, Velázquez *Portrait of a Man*, and Caravaggio's *St. John* and *The Fortune Teller*. Several notable works are also to be found in the municipal reception rooms. These include the statues of *Urban VIII* by Bernini and of *Innocent X* by Algardi, *Boy Removing a Thorn* (1ˢᵗ century B.C. bronze), and the celebrated Etruscan *Capitoline Wolf* (6ᵗʰ-5ᵗʰ century B.C.), a bronze statue of a she-wolf that has been the symbol of Rome for centuries. The twins were added by Antonio del Pollaiolo in the 15ᵗʰ century. The **Capitoline Museum** hosts another collection of Greek and Roman art. It contains such celebrated works as the *Capitoline Venus*, copy of a Hellenistic statue, and the *Dying Gaul*, marble copy of a bronze original of the school of Pergamon (3ʳᵈ cent. B.C.), held by some to be one of the finest pieces of sculpture of antiquity. Two rooms contain busts of emperors, philosophers and poets. Another exceptional example of Roman sculpture is the bronze *statue of Marcus Aurelius* now in a room to the right of the courtyard.

▲ *Bust of Commodus-Hercules*,
2ⁿᵈ cent. A.D.

◄The *Dying Gaul*, one of the finest
sculptures of the ancient world

▲ Triton Fountain,
by Gian Lorenzo Bernini

Triton Fountain

This celebrated fountain, designed by Bernini in 1643,
stands in the middle of bustling
Piazza Barberini. It consists of a
triton (merman) blowing a conch
and standing on an open oyster,
which four dolphins hold aloft on
their tails. The tails also bear the
emblem of Pope Urban VIII Barberini.

Piazza del Popolo

▲ The scenic Piazza del Popolo

The broad elliptical piazza between the 16th century **Porta del Popolo** and the meeting point of Via del Babuino with Via del Corso was designed in the early 1800s by Giuseppe Valadier, who built a lovely fountain at either end. At the center is the *Flaminian Obelisk* (12th century B.C.) formerly in the Circus Maximus and moved here in 1589. The Renaissance **Church of Santa Maria del Popolo** contains various works of art, including two of Caravaggio's masterpieces, the *Conversion of Saint Paul* and the *Martyrdom of* *Saint Peter*, c. 1602, and the **Chigi Chapel**, designed by Raphael. Stairs lead from the square to the top of the Pincio with a magnificent view.

Trevi Fountain

▼ Trevi Fountain

This monumental fountain alone occupies most of Piazza di Trevi, a charming square off **Via del Corso**. It rises on the spot where the Aqua Vergine, the aqueduct built by Agrippa in 19 B.C., had its terminus. After centuries of abandon, the aqueduct was reactivated when, in the 1400s, Pope Nicholas V commissioned Leon Bat-

◄ The pediment of the Trevi fountain with allegoric figures and the coat of arms of Clement XII

►▲▼The colossal statue
of the god *Oceanus*
and detail of the *sea horses*
and *tritons*

tista Alberti to design a basin where
its waters could be collected. The
decorative elements (niches, sculpture, rocks, etc.) were added in the
18th century by Nicola Salvi, who
received the commission from
Pope Clement XII. An imposing
figure of the god *Oceanus* riding
a gigantic seashell drawn by sea-
horses dominates the elaborate
naturalistic architectural setting
in which other figures (tritons) loll
among the rocks. Tiers of steps
run around the great basin.

▲ The famous Spanish Steps
and the Church of Trinità dei Monti
with the Obelisco Sallustiano

Piazza di Spagna

One of the most popular spots in the city is a picturesque hourglass shaped square. The fountain in the center at its narrowest point is the charming **Fontana della Barcaccia**, designed by Pietro Bernini in 1629. Backdrop are the celebrated **stairs of Trinità dei Monti**

▲ The fountain of the Barcaccia
in Piazza di Spagna

or *Spanish Steps,* built in 1726 by Francesco de Sanctis. At the top are an Egyptian obelisk, the so-called *Obelisco Sallustiano,* and the 16th century facade of the **Church of Trinità dei Monti**.

Tiberine Island

The islet, dedicated by the Romans to the god of medicine, Aesculapius, and designed in the shape of a boat, is now mostly occupied by the 16th century hospital (Ospedale di San Giovanni di Dio). The **Church of St. Bartholomew** opposite it was built in the 17th century. Of the various bridges that connect the isle to the mainland, the **Pons Fabricius**, built in 62 B.C., is still basically intact. The **Pons Cestius**, built in travertine, dates to 46 B.C., while all that remains of the **Ponte Rotto**, 16th century, is a single span.

▼ Bird's eye view of the Tiberine Island

Piazza Navona

This imposing Baroque stage setting is one of the best-loved and most picturesque sites in Rome. It rises on the site of the **Stadium of Domitian** and is exactly the same size (m. 240 x 65). The square contains three monumental fountains. The **Fontana del Moro** at one end was designed by Bernini (mid-1600s) and built by Antonio Mari, and at the other end the **Fontana del Nettuno**, 19th century. In the middle of the square is the imposing **Fontana dei Fiumi**, one of Bernini's masterpieces. Dated 1651, it represents a cliff with the river gods of the *Ganges, Nile, Danube* and *River Plata* (a river for each continent) seated around it. Opposite is the **Church of Sant'Agnese in Agone**, begun by Carlo and Girolamo Rainaldi and finished by Borromini in 1657.

Piazza del Quirinale

▼ Piazza del Quirinale with the obelisk and the statues of Castor and Pollux at the center, and the Palazzo del Quirinale in the background

The setting of the square is splendid. It rises on the top of the Quirinal Hill, the site of the Roman Temple of Quirinus. Two enormous *statues of Castor and Pollux*, taken from the Baths of Constantine, stand at the center at the base of a tall obelisk. On one side of the square is the **Palazzo della Consulta**, the seat of Italy's Supreme Court. It was built by Ferdinando Fuga in 1734 as a courthouse for the *Tribunale della Consulta*. The coat-of-arms crowning the facade is the emblem of Clement XII who commissioned the building. The majestic **Palazzo del Quirinale** is the work of several architects, including Mascherino, Fontana, Carlo Maderno, and Bernini. Begun in 1574, it was not completed until around 1735. Formerly a summer residence for the popes, after the unification of Italy at the end of the 19th century it was used as the royal palace. It is now the official residence of the President of the Republic. Inside are works by Guido Reni and Melozzo da Forlì.

▼ The *Pantheon*, in an engraving by Pietro Datri (19th cent.)

Pantheon

This remarkable domed building has survived almost two thousand years of history virtually intact. The original rectangular temple built by Augustus' son-in-law Agrippa in 27 B.C. was turned into the porch of the present-day building when, in 120 A.D., Hadrian had it enlarged. The sixteen majestic columns in the porch have Corinthian capitals. The diameter of the circular interior is equal to its height (43.3 meters). Large niches, with Corinthian columns and pilaster strips, alternate with shrines. The hemispherical dome consists of five tiers of coffering with a large circular opening, 9 meters in diameter, at the center. Dedicated by the ancient Romans to "all the gods", the Pantheon became the solemn mausoleum of Italian kings, queens and artists. Originally, gilded bronze adorned both the pediment and the interior of the porch, but in the 17th century Pope Urban VIII Barberini had the facing removed so that Bernini could use it for the canopy he was constructing in St. Peter's (whence the Roman saying, "*quod non fecerunt barbari, fecerunt Barberini*" which translated means, more or less: "where the barbarians failed, the Barberini prevailed").

San Giovanni in Laterano

The oldest church in Christendom, the Lateran Basilica has been the Cathedral of Rome for almost 20 centuries. The striking main facade designed by Alessandro Galilei in 1735 marks the mid-

▲ The exterior and the interior of the Pantheon

◄ The facade
of San Giovanni in Laterano

▲ The organ, in the right arm
of the transept

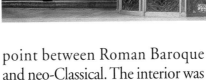

► The sanctuary of the Basilica

▼ The Scala Santa

point between Roman Baroque and neo-Classical. The interior was partially remodeled by Francesco Borromini, who reorganized the imposing nave and double-aisle section in 1650, although he left the transept dating to the preceding century unaltered. The superb *tabernacle* in the transept is a mid-14th century work by Giovanni di Stefano. The **Baptistery**, with entrance from **Piazza San Giovanni in Laterano,** is detached from the church. Its origins date back to Constantine and it has retained its original octagonal form. The marbles and semi-precious stone inlays inside however date to the 17th century. Traces of early medieval walls are visible on one flank.

Santa Maria Maggiore

Of the great basilicas of Rome, Santa Maria has best preserved its original Early Christian structure. Its 75-meter Romanesque bell tower (dated 1377) is the tallest in the city. The facade with five arches and a loggia was designed in 1750 by Ferdinando Fuga. The superb mosaics inside the loggia were part of the original late 13th century facade. The Baroque rear facade, by Ponzio, Rainaldi and Fontana (1676), is also imposing. The stately interior with a nave and two aisles has fine Ionic columns. The Cosmatesque floor mosaics date to the 12th century while the fine coffered ceiling, early 16th century, has been attributed to Giuliano da Sangallo. The mosaic decoration is truly remarkable: the 36 panels on the walls and those on the arch of the nave date to the 5th century; those in the great apse conch, of great beauty, date to 1295 and were designed by Jacopo Torriti.

▲ The Basilica
of Santa Maria Maggiore

San Pietro in Vincoli

The church is also known as the **Basilica Eudoxiana** as it was commissioned by Eudoxia the wife of Emperor Valentinian III in the

▼ The bronze urn containing
Saint Peter's chains

◄ The portico with five arches
in front of the facade
of San Pietro in Vincoli

▶ *Moses*, by Michelangelo, detail of the Tomb of Julius II

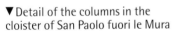

early 5th century. The *chains* still preserved inside the church are those that bound St. Peter when he was confined in the Mamertine Prison in Rome miraculously fused with those that bound him in Palestine. The five-arch portico was commissioned by Giuliano della Rovere and designed by Meo del Caprino around 1475. The church how-ever is best known for Michelangelo's great marble *Moses*, located in the right transept. It was to have been part of the large ensemble of figures on the **Tomb of Julius II** and was to have been set in St. Peter's in the Vatican. Michelangelo spent three years on the project, from 1513 to 1516, but Leo X, who succeeded Julius II, removed the artist from the project. Most of the work was completed by pupils.

San Paolo fuori le Mura

The second largest basilica in Rome was founded in the 4th century on the site of St. Paul's tomb. Remodeled over

▼ Detail of the columns in the cloister of San Paolo fuori le Mura

▶ The facade of San Paolo fuori le Mura

the centuries, it burned down completely in 1823 and was subsequently rebuilt in its original size (132 x 65 meters), preceded by a great porticoed atrium. The imposing interior is adorned with a frieze of *mosaic portraits of popes*. The majestic **triumphal arch** at the end of the nave is a fairly faithful replica of the original, and the mosaics are original (albeit restored). The arch was called the **Arch of Galla Placidia** as it was supposedly commissioned by the Byzantine empress. A notable *ciborium* by Arnolfo di Cambio (1285) and the *apse mosaic* recall the artistic quality of the original church. The remarkable cloister is by the Vassalletto family (1214).

▲ The imposing interior of San Paolo fuori le Mura

Santa Maria in Cosmedin

▼ Remains of the original decoration in the cloister of San Paolo fuori le Mura

Founded in the 6th century, the church was restored in the 12th century. An elegant Romanesque bell tower stands at one side. The inside has a fine floor, a baldachin and a *schola cantorum* (choir), all in Cosmatesque work. In the porch is the **Bocca della Verità** (literally, mouth of truth), a stone disk representing a face, which probably served as a drain covering. According to popular belief, a liar who dares put his hand in the mouth will have it bitten off.

►▲ The Church of Santa Maria in Cosmedin with its Romanesque bell tower and the "Bocca della Verità" in the porch

Santa Cecilia in Trastevere

▼ Church
of Santa Cecilia in Trastevere

The original church was founded before the 5th century on the site of a Roman dwelling (perhaps the home of Cecilia, a 2nd century Roman martyr). Rebuilt by Paschal I in the 9th century, it has since been renovated several times. In the sanctuary is an exceptional *ciborium* (1283) by Arnolfo di Cambio while Stefano Maderno's famous *statue of St. Cecilia* is under the altar. The magnificent large mosaic in the apse dates to the time of Paschal I, who is shown there still alive. Perhaps the most celebrated of all is the *Last Judgment* fresco in the adjoining convent, with a famous depiction of *Christ the Savior,* painted by Pietro Cavallini in 1293; it is unfortunately now in poor condition.

San Carlo alle Quattro Fontane

Located at the intersection of **Via del Quirinale** and **Via delle Quattro Fontane**, this small church is consecrated to the Holy Trinity and St, Charles Borromeo. Since it is very small, the Romans call it **San Carlino**, the small San Carlo. It was designed by the great North Italian architect, Francesco Castelli, known as Borromini, whose Roman career began and ended right here. The plan of the church was drawn up in 1638. It was the first time that Borromini, who up to then had always collaborated with Carlo Maderno, worked on his own. His design was quite original as the idea was to transfer the shape and size of the base of one of the piers of the dome of St. Peter's to the plan of the church. The boldly curving facade, on the other hand, was the last project carried out by the artist, who committed suicide in 1667. Of particular note are the dome and the lantern, as well as the interior decorations (marble columns, gold and stucco), all designed by Borromini.

▲ Church of San Carlo alle Quattro Fontane

San Pietro in Montorio

▼ The facade of San Pietro in Montorio

The **Church of San Pietro in Montorio** stands on the Hill of the Janiculum. It was rebuilt at the end of the 15th century on a 9th century church that stood on the site where Saint Peter was supposedly crucified. Inside are works by Sebastiano del Piombo and Bartolomeo Ammannati. At the center of the cloister, to the right of the church, is the **Tempietto** by Donato Bramante, one of the most important Renaissance architects. Designed in 1502, it was finished around 1510. This central-plan building supplies us with an example of Bramante's interpretation of the antique, of his ideal of the classic, which he subsequently transferred to his project, never carried out, for the reconstruction of the Vatican basilica. The Tempietto consists of a cir-

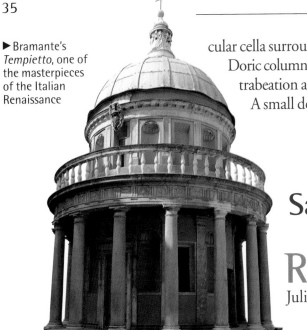

▶ Bramante's *Tempietto*, one of the masterpieces of the Italian Renaissance

cular cella surrounded by sixteen Doric columns supporting the trabeation and a balustrade. A small dome crowns the building. The hole in which, according to tradition, *Saint Peter's cross* was set can be seen in the crypt below the Tempietto.

Santa Maria in Trastevere

Reputedly founded by Pope Julius I around the year 340, Santa Maria in Trastevere is one of the oldest churches in Rome, and the first known church dedicated to the Virgin. Like many others, it was remodeled and restored over the centuries, although the greatest damage was done in the 19th century when mediocre murals were painted on the walls and figures believed to be pagan were removed from some of the capitals. The facade dates to the 12th century with a 13th century mosaic by Pietro Cavallini. The portico was commissioned from Carlo Fontana in 1702 by Pope Clement XI. The statues atop the railing are 16th century, while the bell tower still retains much of its 11th century Romanesque appearance. The same juxtaposition of styles and centuries is repeated inside the church. Of note are the mid-12th century mosaics decorating the apse. Those recounting *episodes from the Life of Mary* were designed by Pietro Cavallini, about whom we know very little, and whose works have mostly been lost. All that is left in Rome is the Saint Cecilia cycle and these mosaics. He was also greatly admired by his contemporaries, and seems to have known Giotto.

▼ The Church of Santa Maria in Trastevere

Via Appia Antica

▲ Porta San Sebastiano

◀ The Appian Way

▼ Tomb of Cecilia Metella

The famous road dates back to the beginning of Roman history. It was repeatedly lengthened until it reached Brindisi (on the east coast), a major port for trade with the Orient. Originally, the road started from **Porta Capena** (hardly any of which is extant today). When the **Aurelian Walls** were built, its starting point was moved to the new city gates, at the time known as **Porta Appia** and later **Porta San Sebastiano**. The Appian Way is the best-preserved of the consular roads. The first few miles are lined with tombs and remains of monuments. One of the few ruins that has been identified is the **Tomb of Cecilia Metella** at kilometer three. The cylindrical tower in travertine was transformed into a fort in the Middle Ages, when the crenellations were added.

▼ Detail of the fresco in the Catacombs of St. Sebastian

Catacombs

The catacombs or *"coemeteria"*, i.e. dormitories, were the burial places of the Christians. The only one to bear the name Catacombs was the cemetery of San Se- bastiano on the Via Appia. In the hybrid Greco-Roman langue of the Christians this indicated its site at the bottom of a trough. The *Catacombs of Domitilla,* also known as the catacombs of St. Nereus and Achilleus, are among the largest in Rome. Perhaps they were orig-

▲ Entrance to the Catacombs
of Domitilla

the Flavians. In the catacombs is the 4th century **Basilica of Saints Nereus and Achilleus,** a three-aisled church with superb Corinthian columns. The most noteworthy tombs include the **hypogeum of the Flavians** with 1st century A.D. murals and the **cubicle of St. Petronilla.** Only a tiny part of the **Catacombs of St. Callistus,** also along the Appian Way, has been explored. Built in the 2nd century A.D. on four levels, they served as the official burial grounds for the first bishops of Rome. The **Crypt of the Popes** contains the tombs of several pontiffs including that of Sixtus II, murdered in the persecutions of the Emperor Valerian in 258.

inally used as the private burial grounds of prominent Christians, among whom Domitilla. As niece of the Emperor Domitian, she belonged to the imperial family of

► Fresco with the *Face of Christ*
(Catacombs of St. Callistus)

▼ One of the corridors
in the Catacombs

Borghese Gallery

► The premises
of the Borghese Gallery

This rich private collection, housed in a charming 17th century building, the **Casino Borghese**, became property of the Italian State in 1902. A few of the many noteworthy works of art include *Pauline Borghese* (Napoleon's sister) portrayed as Venus Victrix, Canova's celebrated sculpture of 1805. One of the foremost masterpieces of neo-Classical sculpture, it is also a tour de force of the master's incredible technical skill. *David*, by Bernini, 1624, *Apollo and Daphne*, 1624, Bernini's greatest youthful work; the *Rape of Persephone*, another youthful work by Bernini (1622); the *Deposition* by Raphael (1507) and other of his works; six paintings by Caravaggio, including the *Boy with a Basket of Fruit*, from his early period, *David with the Head of Goliath,* the *Madonna of the Serpents of the Palafrenieri*, one of his absolute masterpieces, dating to 1605-06; *St. Jerome*, one of the artist's last Roman works, a splendid medita-

▲ *Paolina Borghese-Bonaparte*, by Canova

◄ *Boy with a Basket of Fruit,*
by Caravaggio

▲ *Cupid and Psyche*,
by Jacopo Zucchi

tion on saintliness and death, outstanding in the originality of the horizontal composition and the simple, noble figure of the old man. In 1606, Caravaggio was forced to flee Rome when he got involved in a violent tavern brawl that ended with the killing of a rival. After four years of restless wandering about Italy he died, half crazed and feverish, on the beach of Porto Ercole of an attack of malaria.

▲ Bernini's *David*,
in the Borghese Gallery

Museo Nazionale Etrusco di Villa Giulia

The museum contains a collection of pre-Roman archaeological material from Latium. Among the outstanding pieces: a reconstructed *tomb from Cerveteri* (4th century B.C.), *Apollo* and *Heracles,* late 6th century B.C. Etruscan statues from Veii, and the *Sarcophagus of the married couple,* a remarkable Etruscan terracotta sculpture dating from the 6th century B.C. unearthed at Cerveteri. In addition there are dozens of bronze figurines and ceramic vases, including a 5th and a 4th century B.C. *crater,* a 7th century B.C. *oinochoe,* several *cists* (cylindrical containers in bronze for toilette objects) typical of the Palestrina area, among which is the superb 4th century B.C. *Ficoroni Cista,* gold work, ivories and bronzes, all from Palestrina. In the 1950s the museum was reorganized in line with modern exhibition criteria to offer visitors and scholars a complete overview of pre-Roman art.

▶ *Apollo of Veio,* an Etruscan work

▼ The nymphaeum of Villa Giulia with the Aqua Virgo fountain

Galleria Doria Pamphilj

One of the world's major private collections, it was started in the 17th century by Pope Innocent X Pamphilj, continued by his descendants, and, when the Pamphilj line died out, by the Doria family. It is housed in a grandiose Rococo mansion, **Palazzo Doria**, with a Renaissance courtyard. Most of the works are still hanging in the places selected by the original collectors; many are famous masterpieces. Among the Italians: Titian *(Spain Coming to the Aid of Religion* and *Herodiad),* Tintoretto, Correggio, Raphael *(a double portrait),* Caravaggio *(Mary Magda-*

lene, *St. John,* and *Rest on the Flight into Egypt,* a youthful dreamy work still a long way from the shockingly realistic treatment of his mature works), Carracci, Savoldo, Mattia Preti, Parmigianino, and Salvator Rosa. Among the foreign masters, the most important are Velázquez *(Portrait of Innocent X,* dated 1650), Claude Lorrain (five *mythological landscapes),* Rubens *(Portrait of a Franciscan Monk),* Velvet Breughel and many others. Among the sculptures, three *busts of Innocent X* (two by Bernini and one by Algardi) and a *bust of Olimpia Pamphilj*, also by Algardi.

▲ Detail of Caravaggio's *Rest on the Flight into Egypt*

◄ Annibale Carracci's *Rest on the Flight into Egypt*

▼ *Niobid*

Museo Nazionale Romano
(National Roman Museum)

Founded in 1889, it is one of the most complete museums of ancient art in the world. The museum occupies the premises of what was once a monastery and the Baths of Diocletian. The continuous increase in the amount of archaeological ma-

terial and the acquisition of important collections have made it essential to distribute the works to various exhibition sites. The **Baths of Diocletian**, historical premises of the museum, contain an important collection of inscriptions as well as

▶ Detail
of the sarcophagus of Acilia

columns, capitals, sarcophaguses, etc. The *Palazzo Massimo alle Terme*, overlooking the Piazza dei Cinquecento, is the main headquarters for the museum and contains: the *Lancellotti Discobolus*, copy of Myron's famous Discobolus; the *Tiber Apollo* copy of a 5ᵗʰ century B.C. Greek original attributed to Phidias or Kalamis; the *Niobid from the Horti Sallustiani*, exceptional copy of a Greek mid-5ᵗʰ century B.C. original; the *Sarcophagus of Acilia*, second half of the 3ʳᵈ century B.C.; the *Sleeping Hermaphrodite*, copy of a Hellenistic original, and the splendid *frescoes from the Villa of Livia* at Prima Porta (1ˢᵗ century A.D.). The principal works in the **Palazzo Altemps**, a stone's throw from Piazza Navona, include: the *Athena Parthenos*, copy of the famous statue by Phidias in the Parthenon; the

▼ Roman mosaic
with figures of animals

terrible *Galacian about to commit suicide after killing his wife*, copy of a statue of the school of Pergamon, 3ʳᵈ century B.C.; the 5ᵗʰ century B.C. *Ludovisi Throne* with its extraordinary relief decorations.

Palazzo Venezia

▼ Palazzo Venezia, attributed to Leon Battista Alberti

Looming up over Piazza Venezia its crenellations and massive bulk make it look like a medieval castle. It is hard to believe that this is the first example of Renaissance architecture in Rome. We know that the building was commissioned by Cardinal Pietro Balbo (later Pope Paul II) but the name of the architect who designed it in 1455 has not come down to us, although it is sometimes attributed to Leon Battista Alberti, known to have been working for Pope Nicholas V in Rome at the time. In the 16ᵗʰ century, it became the seat of the Embassy of

▼ *Double Portrait,* by Giorgione

▲ *Virgin and Child,* Venetian School

the Republic of Venice in Rome. In the 19th century, it was taken over by the Austrians, and was not returned to the Italian government until 1916. Since the end of World War II, its premises have been occupied by the ***Museo di Palazzo Venezia***, with paintings by Jacopo Sansovino, Paolo Veneziano and Guercino.

Palazzo Barberini

▼ *Judith and Holofernes,* by Caravaggio

A lovely Baroque palace, begun by Carlo Maderno, continued by Borromini and completed by Bernini (1625-1633). It houses the 13th to 18th century section of the ***National Gallery of Ancient Art.*** The painters represented include Simone Martini, Fra Angelico, Filippo Lippi, Lorenzo Lotto, Agnolo Bronzino, Raphael's famous *Fornarina,* El Greco, Tintoretto and Titian, Hans Holbein the Younger's *Portrait of Henry VIII,* a *Judith and Holofernes* by Caravaggio and Pietro da Cortona's majestic fresco of the *Triumph of Divine Providence.*

▶ *Saint Gregory the Great,* by Saraceni

▲ Raphael's famous *Fornarina*

▼ Ara Pacis Augustae

Ara Pacis Augustae

The temple was commissioned by the Senate of Rome to commemorate the *Pax Augustae* (Peace of Augustus) proclaimed by Augustus throughout the empire in 13 B.C. It consists of a sacrificial altar around which is an enclosure adorned with *ornamental friezes and stupendous reliefs of processions.* Inaugurated in 9 B.C., it fell into ruin and was submerged by accumulated earth and rubble in the Middle Ages. Every so often, from the 16th century on, bits and pieces came to light and were scattered in various museums. In 1938 G. Moretti put them all back together and reconstructed the monument, using plaster casts to fill in the few missing parts.

Castel Sant'Angelo

▲ Castel Sant'Angelo, the bridge of the same name and the Angel on the top of the castle terrace

▼ The Courtyard of the Angel or of the Cannon Balls

This massive building, which looks like a medieval castle, is one of the most famous and fascinating buildings in Rome. It stands on the site of **Hadrian's Mausoleum**, maintaining the original floor plan and some of the rooms. Built in 130 A.D. as the emperor's tomb, it had an immense square base on top of which was a circular drum structure. Then, in 271, Aurelian had it remodeled as a fort. Its name, literally, Castle of the Holy Angel, dates from 590 when an angel foretelling the end of a terrible plague epidemic reputedly appeared on its summit. Throughout the Middle Ages, it served as the popes' stronghold-prison, providing convenient shelter in the case of enemy attack. In the 15th century the great corner bastions were added on and the drum, devoid of its marble facing, was raised. A statue of the *angel* was set up to replace that of the emperor on top of the building. (The one there now is an 18th century work). The vast five story interior is an intricate labyrinth of rooms and corridors dating from various periods. Among the most interesting sights are the **spiral staircase** leading to the emperors' burial chamber, the **Courtyard of the Angel**, a picturesque courtyard still containing medieval ammunitions, and the **Armory**, housing an extensive collection of weapons from various places and periods. Another interesting section is the **Papal Suite**, which was remodeled and sumptuously refurbished by various artists for Pope Paul III, and lastly, the terrace, with a magnificent view over the city.

THE VATICAN

◀ Via della Conciliazione

The Vatican City is the capital of Christianity, headquarters of the Holy Pope, successor of Peter and Vicar of Christ. With an extraordinary wealth of spirituality and art condensed in what amounts to a mere handkerchief of land, the Vatican City is also the smallest state in the world. It covers the Vatican Hill lying between Monte Mario and the Janiculum. In the 1st century A.D. it was the site of Caligula's circus where Nero had hundreds of Christians martyred some years later. One of them was Saint Peter, crucified in 67, and on whose burial site the most important basilica of the Christian world was founded. It developed as an autonomous state in the early Middle Ages and its importance grew till it covered practically all central Italy until it was wiped off the political scene with the unification of Italy. It was not until 1929 under the terms of the Lateran Pact agreement signed with the Italian government that it regained an independent political status as state with an area of less than one fifth of a square mile.

◀ A fountain in Piazza San Pietro

Piazza San Pietro (St. Peter's Square)

One of the most splendid pieces of architecture of all times, the piazza is Gian Lorenzo Bernini's absolute masterpiece. **Via della Conciliazione**, the uninspiring rhetorical boulevard leading to the square, was built in 1937 to create a scenic approach to the monumental complex of St. Peter's. Bernini framed the square, a perfect elliptical shape, 240 meters wide, with two wings of a majestic colonnade (1656-1667). It is composed of 284 columns arranged in four rows and surmounted by 140 *statues of saints and martyrs*. On either side are grandiose **fountains** designed by Carlo Maderno. The Egyptian *obelisk* in the center, brought to Rome from Heliopolis by Caligula to adorn his circus,

▲ St. Peter's Square

was set up on its present site in 1586 – an undertaking so arduous that, according to the records, it took over four months and required the efforts of over one thousand men. A relic of the Cross is at the top of the obelisk.

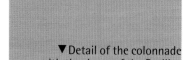

▼ Detail of the colonnade
with the dome of the Basilica

▲ Facade of St. Peter's Basilica

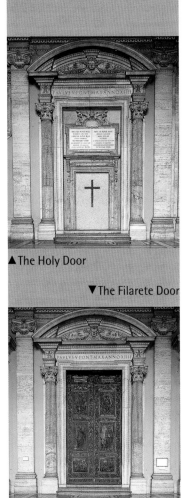

▲ The Holy Door

▼ The Filarete Door

St. Peter's Basilica

The greatest church in Christendom originated in 324 as a shrine for the mortal remains of St. Peter. The building we see today took hundreds of years to complete. The earliest version of the basilica had a five aisle plan with a porch and mosaic decoration on the facade. In the 15th century, when the building's stability was threatened, Nicholas V had it tom down, and commissioned Bernardo Rossellino to design a new one. When Nicholas V died, work was suspended and the project was not resumed until 1506 when Bramante, commissioned by Julius II, took up the work. He was succeeded by Raphael, Antonio da Sangallo, Peruzzi, and Michelangelo. Michelangelo designed the gigantic dome, the biggest ever built, in 1547, basing himself

partially on Bramante's own plans and inspired by Brunelleschi's dome on the Florence cathedral. It was finished sixteen years later by Domenico Fontana and Giacomo Della Porta. In the 17th century, Carlo Maderno was commissioned to enlarge the church, which he did by lengthening the nave – thereby reshaping the ground plan into a Latin cross. Maderno's imposing facade was erected in 1614. A porch decorated with statues of popes precedes the church proper, which has five entrance portals. The one on the far right, the **Holy Door,** is opened only on occasion of Holy Year celebrations, the middle one, the **Filarete Door,** boasts superb bronze reliefs cast by Filarete in 1433, while the one on the far left, the **Death Door,** is the work of a

▲ Apse of St. Peter's

▶ The interior of St. Peter's, with the imposing bronze *Baldachin* by Bernini

▲ Bronze statue of Saint Peter

contemporary Italian master, Giacomo Manzù (1964). The interior conveys an impression of remarkable harmony despite truly gigantic dimensions (length: 210 m., width at the transepts: 137 m., height at the nave: 44 m., dome height: 136 m.). Eight pairs of immense piers line the nave. By the last one on the right-hand side is a *bronze effigy of St. Peter*. The much-venerated statue, dated around the middle of the 13th century, has been attributed to Arnolfo di Cambio. In the left aisle is the fine *tomb of Innocent VIII* by Antonio del Pollaiolo (1498), while opposite, in the first chapel on the right aisle is Michelangelo's marvelous *Pietà*. Sculpted when the master was only twenty-five years old for a French prelate, it is the sole work that bears his signature and was placed here in 1749. Beneath the dome (which can be climbed for a marvelous panorama) are the *Pope's Altar* and Maderno's *Chapel of the Confession,* a semicircular area surrounded by an altar rail where ninety-nine perpetual lights are kept burning above *St. Peter's Tomb*. Above the altar is the impressive bronze *Baldachin,* to which Bernini gave the shape of a processional canopy (in lieu of the more traditional ciborium) sustained by magnificent twisted columns (1624-1633). In the tribune is another of Bernini's striking Baroque creations, the gilded bronze *Throne of St. Peter* (1656-1665), flanked by two superb tombs. On the left is the *tomb*

of Paul III designed by Guglielmo Della Porta in 1575, while on the right is Bernini's *tomb of Urban VIII* dated 1647. Four colossal statues adorn the dome piers. (The *St. Longinus* holding a spear is also by Bernini.) In the right transept is the *tomb of Clement XIII* of 1792, one of Canova's masterpieces; in the left transept is the *tomb of Alexander VII,* dated 1678, a late work by Bernini. In the adjoining chapel is a fine marble altarpiece depicting *St. Leo's encounter with Attila* sculpted by Algardi in 1650. Other notable works are preserved in the **Museum and Treasure-vault of St. Peter's.** The most significant include: a *ciborium* by Donatello (1432), the *tomb of Sixtus IV,* a masterpiece of Renaissance sculpture executed by Antonio del Pollaiolo in 1493, and the fine 4th century *sarcoph-*

agus of Junius Bassus. In the underground chambers, the so-called **Grotte Vaticane,** entered from a pillar of the dome, are tombs of other popes.

▲ Michelangelo's dome, from inside

◄ *Pietà,* by Michelangelo

◄ Saint Peter's Throne, masterpiece by Bernini, in the tribune

▲ *Discobolus* (Museo Chiaramonti)

▼ *Belvedere Torso*
(Museo Pio-Clementino)

Vatican Museums

The incredible Vatican collections (the antique collection is the largest in the world) occupy part of the **Vatican Palaces**, a complex of buildings comprising over 1400 rooms and 20 courtyards. The *Museo Pio Clementino,* containing the highlights of the Vatican's Greek and Roman collection, includes: the celebrated *Belvedere Torso,* perhaps representing Hercules, a late 1st century B.C. work by Apollonius of Nestor which was unearthed in the 15th century and was much admired by Michelangelo; *Meleager,* a Roman copy of a 4th century B.C. sculpture by Scopas; *Apollo killing a Lizard; Satyr at rest,* and *Venus of Cnidus,* all Roman copies of Praxiteles, 4th century B.C. originals; *Sleeping Ariadne,* a refined 2nd century B.C. Hellenistic work; the *Wounded Amazon,* Roman copy of a Phidias original (5th century B.C.); the *Laocoön,* a celebrated marble group dating from the late Hellenistic

period (1st century B.C.-1st century A.D.); the extraordinary *Belvedere Apollo,* a Roman copy of a 4th century original by Leocares, and *Athlete grooming himself,* a Roman copy of a 4th century B.C. work by Lysippus. The *Museo Chiaramonti*: two great masterpieces, the *Prima Porta Augustus,* a late 1st century B.C. Roman work, and the *Doryphorus or Spear-Holder,* a Roman copy of a 5th century B.C. work by Polycleitus.

The *Pinacoteca Vaticana,* erected for Pope Pius XI by the architect Luca Beltrami, houses the Main Offices, the storeroom, the restoration laboratory and sixteen rooms in which 460 works are on exhibit, including: Giotto's magnificent *Stefaneschi Altarpiece,* commissioned in 1300 for the main altar of the old basilica of St. Peter's, paintings by Fra Angelico

► *Sleeping Ariadne*
(Museo Pio-Clementino)

(scenes from the life of St. Nicholas, predella), Melozzo da Forlì's *Sixtus IV and Platina,* detached fresco, and the famous eight lovely *Music-Making Angels* by the same artist, ten stupendous tapestries woven in Brussels in 1516 on cartoons by Raphael, formerly in the Sistine Chapel, Raphael's *Virgin of Foligno,* 1513, commissioned as an ex-voto offering by a prelate in the entourage of Julius II, *The Transfiguration,* Raphael's last work and by some judged his finest, dated 1520, and the *Coronation of the Virgin* with its predella which, instead, was painted by the master in 1503 when he was only twenty; Leonardo's *St. Jerome,* unfinished but remarkably effective; Giovanni Bellini's marvelous *Pietà* (c. 1474); Caravaggio's tragic and telling *Descent from the Cross* of 1604, formerly in Santa Maria in Vallicella. There are also works by Gentileschi, Van Dyck, Pietro da Cortona, Rubens, Poussin; portraits by Titian (*Doge Niccolò Marcello*), Thomas Lawrence (*George IV of England*), Maratta (*Portrait of Clement IX*), Crespi and others.

▲ *Crucifixion,* by Lorenzo Monaco (Pinacoteca Vaticana)

▼ *Music-making Angel,* by Melozzo da Forlì (Pinacoteca Vaticana)

▼ *The Madonna of Foligno,* by Raphael (Pinacoteca Vaticana)

Raphael's Stanze

The apartments known as *Stanze* were begun under Nicholas V in the 15th century. In 1508, Pope Julius decided it was time to complete the decoration of the rooms, suspended by Signorelli and Piero della Francesca in the preceding century, and called in a group of artists that included Lorenzo Lotto, Baldassarre Peruzzi and Perugino. When the pope subsequently had the young Raphael try his hand, Julius was so impressed that he fired everyone else and awarded him the commission. The *Stanza dell'Incendio di Borgo* (The Fire in the Borgo) shows Pope Leo IV miraculously putting out a fire in the Borgo district. However, the most famous frescoes, the *Disputation of the Holy Sacrament*, the

▲ *The Liberation of Saint Peter,* by Raphael (Stanza di Eliodoro)

▶ Room of Constantine

▼ *The School of Athens,* by Raphael (Stanza della Segnatura)

School of Athens and *Parnassus* are in the *Stanza della Segnatura.* Whereas the *Disputation* represents the glorification of Catholicism, the *School of Athens,* which shows the greatest philosophers of all times portrayed around Plato and Aristotle, represents the triumph of philosophy. *Parnassus* represents the world of art. Around Apollo and the Muses are Dante, Virgil, Homer, and other great poets. Next come the *Stanza di Eliodoro* (of Heliodorus) and that of *Constantine*, also decorated with splendid frescoes.

▲ *The Punishment of Korah*
by Sandro Botticelli

◄General view
of the Sistine Chapel

▼General view
of the ceiling of the Sistine Chapel

Sistine Chapel

The conclave of cardinals meets to elect the new pope here, beneath Michelangelo's stirring frescoes. The earliest frescoes, those along the walls, date from 1481. Twelve panels by Perugino and Pinturicchio, Botticelli, Cosimo Rosselli, Signorelli, Ghirlandaio recount the *life of Moses,* on the left, and the *life of Christ*, on the right. Michelangelo, subsequently commissioned by Julius II to decorate the ceiling, carried out the job – without any help – in only four years (1508-1512). The vast iconographic scheme, starting with the *Creation* and continuing up to the *Redemption of Mankind,* is inserted into a complex architectural and decorative framework. The powerful figures of the seven *Prophets* and five *Sibyls* are in the spandrels, while the nine panels in the vault, enclosed in frames and surrounded by beautiful figures of nudes, whose meaning is still not clear, represent:

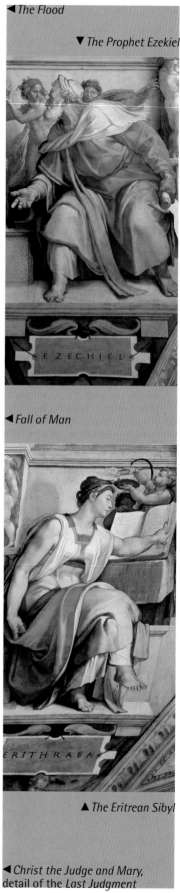

◀ *Fall of Man*

The Separation of Light from Darkness, Creation of Plants, Sun and Moon; Separation of Land from the Sea and Creation of the Birds and Fish, Creation of Adam, one of the most famous paintings of all times; *Creation of Eve, Fall of Man and Expulsion from Paradise,* the most dramatic and also famous, *Noah's Sacrifice, the Flood and the Drunkenness of Noah.* On the end wall is Michelangelo's dramatic *Last Judgment,* painted on a commission from Paul III, more than twenty years later (1536-1541). The complex composition involving 391 figures is wholly dominated by the stern figure of *Christ the Judge,* the focal center of all the action; He is surrounded by the *Blessed* and the *Martyrs* bearing symbols of their martyrdom, while below are *an-*

gels blowing the trumpets of Judgment, with the *Elect Going to Heaven* and, on the right, *Charon sending the Damned to Hell.*

▲ *The Eritrean Sibyl*

◀ *Christ the Judge and Mary,* detail of the *Last Judgment*

Tivoli

Tivoli is situated on a hillside by the banks of the Aniene River, near famous waterfalls. Among the Roman personages who sojourned in the splendid villas built as the patricians' country homes were Julius Caesar, Augustus, and Trajan. Hadrian's Villa, located in the environs, was the most celebrated in ancient Rome. Roman Tivoli was also renowned as the site of numerous temples, although little remains even of the largest which was consecrated to Hercules. It once more became fashionable in the Renaissance, with new villas and parks, but was hard hit by bombs in World War II and much of what we see today is modern.

Hadrian's Villa

The magnificent villa commissioned by Hadrian was built between 118 and 134 A.D. Surrounded by olive groves, of particular note are the *Pecile,* an immense quadriporticus (232 x 97 meters) around a pool, a name derived from an unfounded identification with an Athenian portico; the *Island Nymphaeum,* an elegant circular building, with a portico of Ionic columns and a kind of moat. The tiny villa that once stood on the island inside (today a heap of ruins) is believed to have been Hadrian's personal refuge. The most interesting of the maze-like *Imperial Palace* is the huge peristyle known as *Piazza d'Oro,* an elegant hall known as the *Hall of the Doric Pilasters,* and the *Canopus,* a long narrow pool (119 x 18 meters) in the middle of a natural valley. Near the Canopus is the Museum with numerous statues,

including a fine copy of the *Amazon by Phidias.*

◀▼ **Hadrian's Villa** – Detail with the *Canopus* and the Small Baths

Villa d'Este

This fine 16th century palazzo has what is considered one of the finest examples in the world of the so-called "Italianate gardens". The villa was built between 1550 and 1569 for Cardinal Ippolito II d'Este by the Neapolitan architect Pirro Ligorio. The fine rooms were decorated with frescoes of mythological subjects and views of the villa by Zuccari, Agresti, Muziano and other painters of the Roman school. The park, with a geometrical layout, is famous for its over five hundred fountains, many of which are particularly fascinating, and which blend in with the vegetation.

▲▼ **Villa d'Este** – Viale delle Cento Fontane and the Ovato Fountain

Florence "a new Athens"

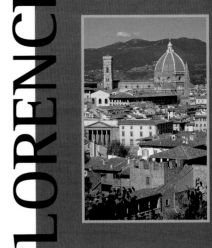

Florence, dubbed "cradle of the Renaissance", "Athens of Italy", and just plain Firenze in Italian, was for over a thousand years a quiet farming town in the Tuscan countryside, both under the Etruscans and as a dominion of the Holy Roman Empire. Its political and economic rise only began around the 11th-12th centuries when, despite warring between the Guelph and Ghibelline factions and recurrent revolts of the populace, fine monuments such as the Baptistery and San Miniato al Monte were built and prosperity from trade paved the way for its future position of leadership. In fact, by the 12th century, when it was a city-state and the first guilds (the famous Corporazioni delle Arti) were already functioning, the Florentine fiorino had become one of the strongest currencies in Europe. The 13th century was the century of Dante Alighieri, whose Divina Commedia written at the beginning of the 14th century in the language spoken by the Florentines and not erudite Latin, laid the basis for modern Italian. In painting, Giotto was the herald of a new style. It was also the century of great public buildings, both secular and religious: the Cathedral and Palazzo Vecchio, both by Arnolfo di Cambio. International Gothic and the school of Giotto, Boccaccio and his Decameron characterized the 1300s. But it was also a time of time of economic hardships, marked by the Black Death and various financial cracks. In 1434, after the fall of the Communal form of government, Cosimo dei Medici, known as the Elder, seized power and marked the beginning of the Medici Signoria. The cultural ferments of Humanism grew ever stronger and reached their zenith in Florence with the Renaissance. Under the patronage of the refined classically oriented Medici court, above all with Lorenzo the Magnificent, there was a flowering of literature (Lorenzo himself, Poliziano, Pulci), of painting (Botticelli, Lippi, Ghirlandaio, Paolo Uccello), architecture (Brunelleschi, Michelozzo, Alberti), sculpture (Donatello,

Verrocchio, della Robbia). Politically Lorenzo successfully succeeded in balancing the various powers, but at the end of the century the Medici were driven out and the citizenry proclaimed the Republic of Florence. Savonarola, Machiavelli, Michelangelo and Leonardo da Vinci were among the prominent figures of this period. In the sixteenth century the Medici returned and the grand duke Cosimo I skillfully consolidated Florence's dominions in Tuscan territory. His successor Francesco I put together the first nucleus of the Uffizi collection. The Medici and their successors in 1737, the Lorraine grand dukes, continued to promote artistic endeavors of every sort, encouraging the construction of villas, parks and monumental palaces. The political importance of Florence has however in the meantime greatly declined. The 19th century was characterized by the Risorgimento struggles and the brief period of Florence capital of the Kingdom of Italy (1865-1871). The city however never gave up its role as a lively center for art and culture. Serious damage was inflicted by bombs in World War II and by the disastrous flood of 1966. Today Florence offers tourists from all over the world the elegant image of a city of art, par excellence, with high quality craft products (gold, leather, straw, footwear), genuine gastronomy and the famous wines of the Chianti. The most interesting folklore events include the Scoppio del Carro (at Easter) and Calcio in Costume (May-June). Outstanding also are the performances of the Maggio Musicale and the fashion shows (Pitti-Moda).

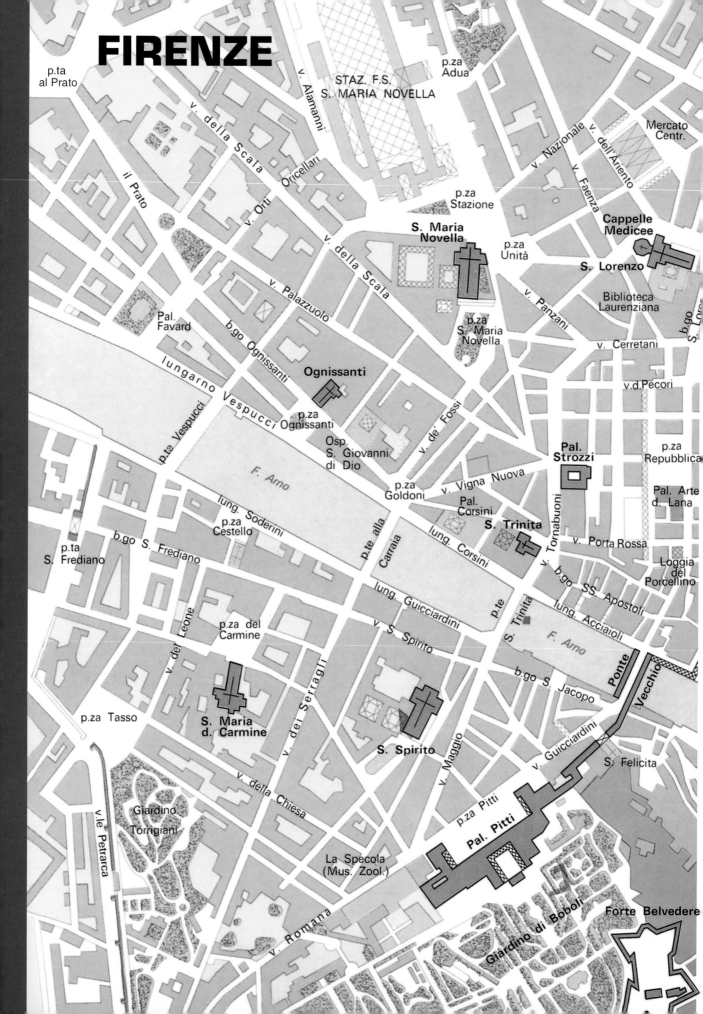

Baptistery

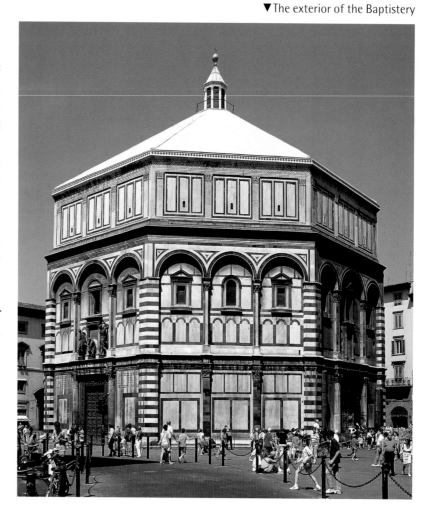

For a certain period of time the Romanesque Battistero di San Giovanni was the cathedral of Florence. Probably built around the 5th century, the Baptistery is a striking eight-sided green and white marble building. The sculpted doors on three sides are celebrated works: the **South door** with *Scenes from the life of St. John the Baptist* by Andrea Pisano (1330), the **North door** with *Scenes from the New Testament* by Ghiberti (1424); the *East door* – one of the great masterpieces of Early Renaissance art – is the **Door of Paradise** sculpted with *Old Testament stories* by Ghiberti. The interior has two architectural orders. These consist of the lower part, which has granite columns with gilded capitals alternating with pillars, and the upper part, between whose smaller pillars are the windows of the so-called women's gallery

◄ The famous Door of Paradise, by Lorenzo Ghiberti

▼ Lorenzo and Vittorio Ghiberti in the frame of the Door of Paradise

▲ The South Door, by Andrea Pisano

▲ The interior of the Baptistery

► The splendid mosaics
in the dome

where the women once sat during religious services, separated from the men. On the triumphal arch of the apse and on the cupola are splendid Byzantine style mosaics carried out in the 13th and 14th centuries by various Venetian and Florentine artists including Cimabue and the "Magdalene Master". The mosaics in the apse were begun in 1225 by Jacopo da Torrita. The overwhelming figure of Christ the Judge, attributed to Coppo di Marcovaldo, is over eight meters high.

Giotto's Bell Tower

▼View of the religious complex and panel with the *Drunkenness of Noah*, from Giotto's bell tower

Giotto started work on the bell tower with its unmistakable Gothic silhouette in 1334, completed after his death by Andrea Pisano and Francesco Talenti. A marvelous view of Florence can be had from the top of the 85-meter tall tower, clad in green, pink and white marble to harmonize with the neighboring monuments. The bas-reliefs on the base were sculpted by Andrea Pisano to designs by Giotto. The originals are now in the *Museo dell'Opera del Duomo*.

Cathedral

The **Cathedral of Santa Maria del Fiore** was begun in 1294 by Arnolfo di Cambio, on the site of the old **church of Santa Reparata** (c. 4th-5th century), not large enough to contain Florence's growing Christian community. Other artists who followed Arnolfo in its construction included Giotto, Francesco Talenti, and Brunelleschi. The present facade was added in the late 19th century by the architect De Fabris. In 1420 Brunelleschi began the remarkable octagonal dome built in brick with marble ribs and topped by a lantern. Of note are the cathedral's lateral portals: the early 15th century **Porta della Mandorla** (north side) and the 14th century **Canon's Door** (south side).

▲ The facade of the Cathedral

▼ One of the four exedras of the Cathedral

▶ The Canons' Door

The feeling of stark majesty pervading the interior is enhanced by the oversize piers that separate the aisles from the nave and by the impressive stained-glass windows (14th-15th century). On the left wall are two celebrated frescoes commemorating 15th century military figures: *Monument to John Hawkwood* painted by Paolo Uccello in 1436 alongside the grisaille *Monument to Niccolò da To-*

▶ The *Last Judgment*, in the vault of the dome, by Giorgio Vasari and Federico Zuccari

▼ The interior of the Cathedral

►*Monument to John Hawkwood*, by Paolo Uccello

▲ *Monument to Niccolò da Tolentino*, by Andrea del Castagno

▲Tomb slabs in the crypt of Santa Reparata

lentino painted by Andrea del Castagno in 1456. On the same side a little further on is a panel depicting *Dante and his Divine Comedy* by Domenico di Michelino (1465). A *Crucifix* by Benedetto da Maiano dated 1497 adorns the main altar, surrounded by an octagonal choir. The dome is covered by a fresco of the *Last Judgment* by Vasari and Zuccari. Of interest too are the **Sacrestia Vecchia** and the **Sacrestia Nuova**. A flight of stairs in the right aisle leads down to the *Crypt of Santa Reparata* which not only contains remains of the original Florentine cathedral (tombs, frescoes, capitals), but also the recently-discovered *tomb of Brunelleschi*.

Museo dell'Opera del Duomo

The cathedral museum, located in a building behind the apse of the Cathedral, houses works from the adjacent monuments. Its best-known treasure is Michelangelo's *Pietà* (c. 1550). Left unfinished, it is perhaps the most dramatic of Michelangelo's versions of the subject. Other highlights include sculpture by Arnolfo, Donatello, and Nanni di Banco (from the original Cathedral facade), the two Cathedral **Cantorie** (choir-balconies) – one by Luca della Robbia in 1438 and one by Donatello in 1439 –, Donatello's *Mary Magdalene* carved in wood in 1455

▲ Relief with *The Blacksmith's Craft*, from Giotto's bell tower, by Andrea Pisano

◀ *Pietà*, by Michelangelo

▲ *Mary Magdalene*, by Donatello

▶ *Cantoria (choir gallery) (det.)*, by Luca della Robbia

for the Baptistery, relief plaques with the *Activities of Man*, the *Creation of Adam and Eve*, the *Planets* and the *Liberal Arts* by Andrea Pisano and others, from the bell tower; various objects of the minor arts such as reliquaries, vestments, and a fine silver *altar frontal* dating to the 14th-15th century with *Stories of John the Baptist*. The *silver altar cross*, a precious and complex work of Florentine gold craft of the 14th-15th century, is by Betto di Francesco, Antonio del Pollaiolo and Bernardino Cennini. The restored panels of Ghiberti's **Door of Paradise**, removed from the Baptistery in 1990 and replaced by copies, are also on view in the museum.

▲ *Habakkuk*, by Donatello

◀ *Jeremiah*, by Donatello

▼ Silver altarpiece with *Stories of St. John the Baptist* by Verrocchio and others

Orsanmichele

▼ View of Orsanmichele

This imposingly massive building was designed by Arnolfo di Cambio in 1290 as a loggia for the grain merchants. It was built on the site of the old **church of San Michele in Orto** (*orto*=garden), hence the name. Burnt down in 1304, Orsanmichele was completely rebuilt in the 1300s in a mature Gothic style with elegant mullioned windows and arches. The niches on the pillars outside contain the *statues of the Patron Saints of the Guilds* (14th and 15th cents.) by Ghiberti, Nanni di Banco, Donatello, Verrocchio and others. The

▼ *Shrine of the Madonna delle Grazie*, by Andrea Orcagna

interior, decorated with frescoes, sculpture and stained glass, contains the Gothic **Shrine of the Madonna delle Grazie** by Andrea Orcagna (1359), with Bernardo Daddi's panel of the *Madonna*, made in thanksgiving after the 1348 plague came to an end. On the feast day of St. Anne, the 26th of July, each year, the banners of the guilds are hung around the church to commemorate the expulsion of the Duke of Athens from Florence (26 July 1343). A fly-over bridge links Orsanmichele to the **Palazzo dell'Arte della Lana** or Wool Merchants Guild Hall (14th cent.). The Gothic **shrine** on the corner, known as **Santa Maria della Tromba**, contains a painting by Jacopo del Casentino (14th cent.) dedicated to the *Virgin*.

▼ Palazzo dell'Arte della Lana (Wool Guild)

Piazza della Signoria

▲ Civic coats of arms
on the facade of Palazzo Vecchio

From the early 1300s when Palazzo Vecchio was being built to this day, the square has been the scene of all major Florentine political events. In 1498, for instance, it was here that Girolamo Savonarola was burned at the stake. The three great arches of the **Loggia della Signoria**, also known as *Loggia dei Lanzi* because the Medici's Swiss guards, the *Lanzichenecchi,* used to station under it in the 16th cen-

◄▼ The Loggia de' Lanzi
in an old painting
and panorama of Piazza della Signoria

◄The *Rape of the Sabine Women*, by Giambologna ▼ *Perseus*, by Benvenuto Cellini

▼The *Neptune Fountain*, by Bartolomeo Ammannati

tury, and ***Loggia dell'Orcagna*** because it was once erroneously attributed to Orcagna, occupy one of the sides. The loggia was built in the 1380s by Benci di Cione and Simone Talenti as a site for public ceremonies, and later became a sort of open-air sculpture museum when works such as Benvenuto Cellini's *Perseus*, 1554, Giambologna's *Rape of the Sabine Women*, 1583, *Menelaos carrying the dead Patroclus*, a Roman copy of a Greek original, restored by Tacca, were placed under it. *Hercules slaying the Centaur Nessus*, a large and interesting group by Giambologna, was finally placed in the Loggia in 1842 after being displayed in various other places. The **Fountain**, to the left of Palazzo Vecchio, is by Ammannati, with the great statue of *Neptune* (popularly called *Biancone* - big whitey), surrounded by nereids, tritons and sea-horses (1575); left of the fountain is the *equestrian statue of Cosimo I de' Medici,* by Giambologna (1594). A copy of Michelangelo's *David* (the original is in the Accademia Gallery) stands at the entrance to Palazzo Vecchio, as does Baccio Bandinelli's *Hercules and Cacus.* At No. 5 on the Piazza della Signoria, is the **Raccolta Alberto della Ragione,** a small but interesting modern art collection (Campigli, Rosai, De Chirico, etc.).

▲ The *equestrian statue of Cosimo I de' Medici,* by Giambologna

▼ The entrance to Palazzo Vecchio

Palazzo Vecchio

Arnolfo di Cambio designed the building, symbol of Communal Florence, in 1299, and the Tower in 1310. Modifications were made in the 14th-15th centuries and again in the 16th by Vasari and Buontalenti. The distinctive massive building with its rusticated stone facing, two orders of bifores and the *civic coats of arms* in the arches below the balustrade, and with a 16th century frieze with the *monogram of Christ* over the portal looks like an imposing castle with crenellations and tower. The building was the headquarters of the institutions of the Commune during the Middle Ages, then those of Cosimo I in the 16th century and

of the Italian Chamber of Deputies between 1865 and 1871. It is now Florence's city hall. The portal leads into the main courtyard designed by Michelozzo (15th century), with a **fountain with putto** by Verrocchio of 1476 at the center (copy, the original is in the Cancelleria), and with frescoes and stuccoes by Vasari on the walls. A great staircase leads to the first floor with the immense **Salone dei Cinquecento** or Hall of the 500, designed by Cronaca in 1495, decorated by Vasari and assistants around the mid-1500s with paintings and tapestries. Michelangelo's statue of *Victory* (1534) is part of the sculptural

decoration. Off the hall is the **Studiolo of Francesco I**. Designed by Vasari and the Humanist scholar Borghini in 1572 for Francesco's collections of rarities, it was decorated by the foremost Mannerist artists of the 16th century. On the same floor, are the **Quartiere del Mezzanino** by Michelozzo, now housing the *Loeser Collection,* featuring 14th-16th century Tuscan

◄ *Victory*, by Michelangelo

▲ Michelozzo's courtyard and the putto, detail of Verrocchio's fountain

▼ The Salone dei Cinquecento

▶ *Judith and Holofernes,*
by Donatello

◀ *Hercules and Diomedes,*
by Vincenzo de' Rossi

painting and sculpture and the **Sala dei Duecento** (Hall of the 200) designed by the Maianos in 1477. On the upper floor are the Medici apartments: the **Quartiere di Eleonora di Toledo** (Cosimo I's wife) designed by Vasari, with a delightful chapel decorated by Bronzino, the **Quartiere degli Elementi**, again by Vasari and assistants; the striking **Sala dei Gigli** with a ceiling by Giuliano da Maiano, a carved portal by Benedetto da Maiano, frescoes (including one by Ghirlandaio late 15th century), and a splendid bronze by Donatello (c 1455) of *Judith and Holofernes*. The **Cancelleria** contains a *bust of Niccolò Machiavelli* who had his office here. The **Wardrobe Room**, designed to house part of the treasures of the Medici family in the cupboards along its walls, now contains the 53 magnificent *geographical and nautical maps,* of considerable historical importance, painted by Ignazio Danti and Stefano Buonsignori between 1563 and 1575.

▼ The Sala dei Gigli

Uffizi Gallery

The building was commissioned in the 1560s by Cosimo I as offices *(uffizi)* from which to administer the affairs of state of his domain, the Grand Duchy of Tuscany.

Vasari, the architect picked by Cosimo, came up with a design consisting of two porticoed wings joined by a short arch that opened out onto the river. A few years later (1565) he completed a second project, the Corridoio Vasariano, a long corridor which runs from the Uffizi, crosses the river along the Ponte Vecchio, and ends half a kilometer away at Palazzo Pitti. The Uffizi was turned into an art gallery by Bernardo Buontalenti in 1582 for Cosimo's son Francesco I. Buontalenti reorganized the rooms,

▲ *Holy Family* known as the "Doni Tondo", by Michelangelo

◄ Piazzale degli Uffizi at night

▼ The Uffizi loggia overlooking the Arno

▼ *Ognissanti Madonna*, by Giotto

▲ *Rucellai Madonna*, by Duccio

and also added some new elements, e.g., the striking Tribuna. The collection, enriched over the years by Francesco's successors, became property of the state in 1737 when the last of the Medicis, Anna Maria Ludovica, left it to the City of Florence.

To mention only a few of the principal works: the three altarpieces of the *Virgin Enthroned (Maestà)* by Cimabue, Giotto, and Duccio; the elegant *Annunciation* by Simone Martini and Lippo Memmi; Starnina's detailed *Thebaid*; Gentile da

▼ *Thebaid*, by Starnina

◄ Battle of San Romano, by Paolo Uccello

Fabriano's rich *Adoration of the Magi;* the telling *Portraits of Battista Sforza and Federico da Montefeltro* by Piero della Francesca; the *Badia polyptych* from the church of that name by Giotto; the extraordinary *Battle of San Romano* by Paolo Uccello; the *Madonna and Child* by Filippo Lippi; the famous masterpieces by Botticelli, *Primavera,* the *Birth of Venus,* the *Madonna of the Pomegranate,* and many others. Botticelli described as no one else the elegant and sophisticated Florence of the 15th century, at times with a languid touch, at times with a melodic line of incomparable beauty, at times with the unexpected dramatic violence

▲ Portrait of Battista Sforza, by Piero della Francesca

▼ Madonna and Child with two angels, by Filippo Lippi

▲ Madonna of the Goldfinch, by Raphael

► *Venus of Urbino*, by Titian

▼ *Portrait of
Federico da Montefeltro,*
by Piero della Francesca

of his late works. The allegories, tondos, mythological scenes in the Uffizi are a unique collection of Botticelli's oeuvre. Then there are the *Portinari Altarpiece,* by Hugo van der Goes; three works by Leonardo da Vinci including the *Annunciation;* the *Doni Tondo* by Michelangelo; the sweet *Madonna of the* *Goldfinch* and *Portrait of Leo X,* by Raphael; Titian's *Venus of Urbino;* and works by Caravaggio, Pontormo, Rubens, Van Dyck, Giorgione, Dürer, Goya, Canaletto and the self-portraits in the **Corridoio Vasariano**. The *"Tribune"* of the Uffizi was built on an octagonal plan by Buontalenti (1585-89) in order to create

▼ *Birth of Venus,*
by Sandro Botticelli

▲ *Annunciation*, by Leonardo da Vinci

▼ The Tribuna of the Uffizi

a setting for the gallery's most precious and greatly admired works. The cupola was decorated with mother-of-pearl shells by Poccetti. Among the various marble groups exhibited here, the most outstanding is the *Medici Venus*, discovered during excavations of Hadrian's Villa

▼ *Baptism of Christ* (det.), by Andrea del Verrocchio and Leonardo da Vinci

◄ *Medici Venus*
(2nd cent. B.C.)

at Tivoli, near Rome, and brought to Florence during the reign of Grandduke Cosimo III. The 17th century *octagonal table*, with its intricate design by Ligozzi and Poccetti, is one of the finest examples of Florentine semi-precious stone inlaid mosaic. It took 16 years to complete.

Ponte Vecchio

A side window of the Uffizi Gallery provides a fine view of the famous bridge reflected in the Arno flowing towards Pisa. The bridge is called Ponte Vecchio ("Old Bridge") because it is the oldest bridge in Florence. Indeed there was a crossing at this point of the Arno as far back as the time of the Etruscans. There is record of a wooden footbridge here in 972. The stone bridge subsequently built was destroyed by a flood in 1333. In 1345 it was rebuilt in stone as it is now, with the shops on either side, by Neri di Fioravante. The shops were once occupied by butchers but in the 16th century they were assigned to gold and silversmiths, by order of Ferdinand I. The famous corridor built by Vasari to link the Uffizi Gallery on one side with the Pitti Palace on the other runs along on high on the left. Traces of the disastrous flood of 1966 can still be detected on the buildings along the left bank. Ponte Vecchio has been closed to vehicular traffic for various years and is an oasis of peace and quiet in the midst of the bustling streets on either side.

▼ Ponte Vecchio

▲▶ Palazzo Pitti and the majestic inner courtyard, by Ammannati

Palazzo Pitti

This remarkable palace was designed by Brunelleschi around the mid-1400s for Luca Pitti, a rich Florentine merchant. Originally the building had three levels of rusticated ashlars and was only seven windows wide (the central windows, over the entrance portal). The Medici family bought the palace and enlarged and altered it, moving there in 1550. At the same time they also had the **Boboli Gardens**, one of the most interesting examples of Italianate gardens, laid out behind the palace to designs by Tribolo. Further transformations occurred in the 17th and 18th centuries. Palazzo Pitti houses exceptionally impor-

tant art collections: the *Palatine Gallery*, which still retains the aspect of a 17th century picture gallery, with a wealth of incredible masterpieces in the magnificent rooms decorated with frescoes by Ciro Ferri and Pietro da Cortona; the *State Apartments*; the *Gallery of Modern Art* with its important nucleus of 19th century Tuscan Macchiaoli, and the *Museo degli Argenti* or Silver Museum with its precious works in gold and silver, glass and gems. Some of the principal works in the

▼ *Rooster*, German goldsmith's work in the Museo degli Argenti

▼ Entrance to the fountain
of the Ocean in the Boboli Gardens

▶ The Grotta Buontalenti
in the Boboli Gardens

▼ The Queen's Room in the State Apartments

Palatine Gallery are: *Portrait of a Woman* known as *La Bella*, the *Magdalene* and *Portrait of a Man in Black*, all by Titian; *Peasants Returning from the Fields, The Four Philosophers*, and *The Consequences of War* by Rubens; *La Velata* by Raphael. Her very feminine and serene beauty is accented by her splendid gray silk dress lined with old gold. Her mysterious smile and the position of her hands vaguely recalls Leonardo's Mona Lisa. The *Madonna of the Grand Duke* and the *Madonna of the Chair* are also by Raphael. This famous tondo was painted by Raphael around 1516 in Rome, in the full maturity of his style. He used the woman he loved, Margherita Luti, a woman of the people known as "la Fornarina" (or baker's daughter), as model for Mary. Constantly alive to the world surrounding him, Raphael drew ably upon the experience amassed by the group of artists at work at the papal court, harmonizing the monumental plasticity of Michelangelo with the warm tones of Sebastiano del Piombo, us-

▼ *Magdalene*, by Titian

▲ Portrait of a woman known as *"La Bella"*, by Titian

◀ The *Beautiful Simonetta*, by Botticelli

ing his vision to express a concept of beauty based on harmony of proportions and complete absence of passion. The deeply human and maternal feeling, the brilliant colors and golden flesh tints, the Latin beauty of the faces have earned the painting wide popularity. Other works by Raphael include the *Madonna of the Impannata* (the cloth-draped window), the *Portrait of a Woman* known as *"La Gravida"* (Pregnant woman) and various portraits including those of *Tommaso Inghirami, Agnolo Doni* and *Maddalena Doni*. Other works include portraits by Van Dyck, Velázquez, Sustermans, works by Perugino

▼ *Madonna of the Chair*, by Raphael

▲ *The Consequences of War,*
by Rubens

▼ *Magdalene,* by Perugino

(the enchanting *Magdalene*), Veronese, Botticelli (the *Beautiful Simonetta*), Filippo Lippi (*Madonna and Child*), Tintoretto, Murillo, Salvator Rosa, a series of imaginary landscapes by Flemish and Dutch artists (Van Poelenburg, Ruysch, Schalcken, Brueghel the Elder).

▼ The *Velata* and the *"Gravida"*,
by Raffaello

Santo Spirito

This fine early Renaissance church was begun by Brunelleschi in 1444 and finished by Manetti in 1487. The bell tower is by Baccio d'Agnolo (1517). The interior is a splendid example of Brunelleschi's typical architectural equilibrium: a harmonious linking of spaces, articulated by the regularity of the colonnade, leads to the focal point of the crossing and the dome. Works by Filippino Lippi, Sansovino and Rossellino embellish the church. On the right after leaving is the Cenacolo di Santo Spirito, refectory of the original monastery, frescoed by Orcagna (c. 1360). Palazzo Guadagni, traditionally attributed to Cronaca, stands on the piazza of the same name.

▲View of the Church and of the interior of Santo Spirito

◀The *Nerli altarpiece*, by Filippino Lippi

▼ The facade
of Santa Maria del Carmine

▲ View of the right wall
of the Brancacci Chapel

Santa Maria del Carmine

▼ *Expulsion from Paradise*,
by Masaccio, detail of the left wall

The original church dating from the second half of the 13th century was built for the Carmelite order. Decorated by Giotto, Taddeo Gaddi, Masolino and Masaccio, it was almost completely destroyed by fire in 1771, with the exception of the Corsini and Brancacci Chapels. It was then rebuilt by Giuseppe Ruggeri. The **Corsini Chapel** contains fine Baroque sculpture by Giovan Battista Foggini and the *monument to Saint Andrea Corsini*. The museum with many detached frescoes is also of particular note. Among these is the imposing fresco of the *Last Supper* by Allori. The **Brancacci Chapel** contains the famous cycle of frescoes begun by Masolino (1424-1425),

continued by Masaccio (1426-1427) and finished by Filippino Lippi in 1485. In the *Tribute Money* Masaccio's full genius comes forth. The immobile figures of the Apostles encircle the Savior. This large silent group draws attention to the central part with Christ pointing to the lake where Peter will find the fish with a coin in its mouth with which to pay the tribute. The statuesque figures and the grave dignity of their gestures enhance the nature and importance of man already visible in Giotto and reaffirmed by Michelangelo. Masaccio's inventive power brought new vigor to the art of painting. Botticelli, Leonardo, Michelangelo and many other modern artists such as Carrà and Ottone Rosai have stood in mute admiration before Masaccio's work. Next to the church is the convent, with a fine 17th century cloister with panels by the Florentine painter Guarnieri illustrating the fresco technique.

Santa Maria Novella

The church was built by the Dominicans in the first half of the 13th century. The splendid facade was begun in the 14th century and completed by Alberti the following century (upper section and portal) with geometric marble inlays that recalled Romanesque modules. The entrance to the cloisters is to the left of the facade. The first cloister is the **Chiostro Verde** with 15th century frescoes, together with the restored frescoes by Paolo Uccello (the finest are the *Flood* and the *Sacrifice of Noah*) formerly in the Refectory leading to the cloister. The **Chiostro Grande**, the **Chiostrino dei Morti** and the **Cappellone degli Spagnoli** or Spanish Chapel are entered from the Chiostro Verde. The Spanish Chapel was built in 1350 and used for the religious services of the Spanish entourage of Eleonora of Toledo in the 16th centuries. This large room was entirely frescoed by Andrea di Bonaiuto with scenes from the *History of the Dominican Order and the*

▼ The Church of Santa Maria Novella and detail of the *Birth of the Virgin*, by Domenico Ghirlandaio

▶ *Trinity*, by Masaccio

▲ The magnificent
three-aisled interior

▼ *The Church militant and triumphant*, detail of the Spanish Chapel, frescoed by Andrea di Bonaiuto and assistants

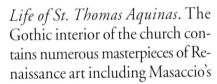

Life of St. Thomas Aquinas. The Gothic interior of the church contains numerous masterpieces of Renaissance art including Masaccio's masterpiece, the *Trinity*, of around 1427 on the wall of the left aisle. A magnificent *Crucifix* on panel by Giotto is in the Sacristy. The raised **Cappella degli Strozzi di Mantova** is decorated with frescoes by Nardo di Cione and an altarpiece by Orcagna. Brunelleschi's famous *Crucifix* is in the first chapel to the left of the high altar. A marvelous fresco cycle by Ghirlandaio with *Stories of the Virgin and John the Baptist* is in the apse. Michelangelo, barely thirteen at the time, learned the rudiments of mural painting from Domenico del Ghirlandaio in the decoration of the apse, teachings that were later to prove invaluable when he was faced with frescoing the Sistine Chapel. Later, as a successful artist, he was to affectionately call this church "my fiancée". Frescoes by Filippino Lippi decorate the first chapel to the right of the main chapel.

▲ View of the Basilica of San Lorenzo

San Lorenzo

Of ancient origins, the church was rebuilt in the 15th century for the Medici by Brunelleschi. The facade was never finished. The interior is extraordinarily harmonious. It contains two fine bronze **pulpits** by Donatello (1460), a *Marriage of the Virgin* by Rosso Fiorentino (1523) at the second right altar, a **shrine** by Desiderio da Settignano (at the end of the right aisle) and an *Annunciation* by Filippo Lippi (left transept). At the center the coffered ceiling of the nave, illuminated by tall windows, bears the coat of arms of the house of Medici. The adjacent **Sacrestia Vecchia** or Old Sacristy was built by Brunelleschi and decorated by Donatello. It contains the *tomb of Giovanni and Piero dei Medici* by Verrocchio. In the square in front of the basilica is a statue of Giovanni dalle Bande Nere, the only real military leader of the Medici family, by Baccio Bandinelli (1540). To the left of the facade of the church is the entrance to the *Laurentian Library*, begun by Michelangelo in 1524 for Pope Clement VII and finished by Vasari and assistants.

▲ Bronze *Pulpit*, by Donatello

Medici Chapels

There are two tomb complexes: the **Cappella dei Principi**, grandiose, entirely faced with marbles and semi-precious stones, with the *tombs of the Grand Dukes*; the

▼ The dome of the Cappella dei Principi and the majestic interior

splendid **Sacrestia Nuova** by Michelangelo (1524), with the *tomb of Giuliano of Nemours*, with the famous statues of *Day* and *Night* and the *tomb of Lorenzo of Urbino* with *Dawn* and *Dusk*. A *Madonna and Child* by Michelangelo is on the *tomb of Giuliano and Lorenzo the Magnificent*. This magnificent masterpiece presents us with Michelangelo architect and sculptor. The two cannot be distinguished for the work must be seen as an inseparable whole, where architecture and sculpture merge and mutually complete each other. The

square room with its imposing dome actually does give a feeling of movement as each architectural element emphasizes the plastic vitality of the forms. The cupola over the apse behind the altar is structurally similar but proportionately smaller.

▲ *Night*, detail of the tomb of Giuliano duke of Nemours, by Michelangelo

▼ *Madonna and Child*, by Michelangelo

▲ The *tomb of Lorenzo duke of Urbino*, by Michelangelo

Palazzo Medici-Riccardi

▲ View of the Palace Chapel

One of the finest examples of Florentine civic architecture of the 15th century, it was built by Michelozzo around 1460 for Cosimo the Elder. Lorenzo the Magnificent later embellished it and in the 17th century it passed to the Riccardi and was enlarged. The outer facing of the building is divided into three horizontal bands: the ground story has heavily rusticated masonry, the intermediate has channeled masonry and the top floor is in plain ashlar masonry. The two upper floors have two-light windows and a ma-

▲ Palazzo Medici-Riccardi

▼ *Procession of the Magi on their Way to Bethlehem,* by Benozzo Gozzoli

jestic cornice crowns the building. The two corner windows, below, are attributed to Michelangelo. Inside, access to the *Museo Mediceo* (where temporary exhibitions are held) is from the left of the porticoed courtyard. Opposite the garden and on the right, a staircase leads to the **Chapel** built by Michelozzo and sumptuously frescoed by Benozzo Gozzoli with the *Procession of the Magi on their Way to Bethlehem* (1460), containing various portraits of the Medici family. Other stairs lead to the gallery, frescoed by Luca Giordano (1683). Lorenzo the Magnificent, Leo X and Clement VII were all born here.

▼ The ceiling of the Gallery of Palazzo Medici-Riccardi frescoed by Luca Giordano

Santissima Annunziata

▼ Piazza della Santissima Annunziata and one of the terra-cotta tondos by Andrea della Robbia on the facade of the Spedale degli Innocenti

B uilt by Michelozzo between 1444 and 1481 on the site of a pre-existing 13th century oratory, the church was completed by Alberti who designed the dome (lining it up with the dome of the Cathe-

▼ One of the fountains by Tacca in the square

▶ *Statue of the Grand Duke Ferdinando I, by Giambologna*

dral along Via dei Servi). The **Spedale degli Innocenti** designed by Brunelleschi and begun in 1419 also overlooks the square. The spandrels between the arches are decorated with glazed terra-cotta tondos of babes in swaddling clothes by Andrea della Robbia. The fountains are by Tacca. In the center of the square is the *equestrian monument to Ferdinando I* by Giambologna.

▼ The *François vase*, masterpiece of Greek ceramics

Archaeological Museum

The museum is housed in the 17th century **Palazzo della Crocetta** and its attractive garden. The collections (established between 1870 and 1880) are distributed among the *Museo Egizio* and the *Antiquarium Etrusco-Greco-Romano*. The Egyptian Museum contains papyri, jewelry, sculpture, mummies and sarcophaguses. Much of the Egyptian material was collected by Ippolito Rosellini in 1829 in the course of a Franco-Tuscan archaeological expedition in Egypt together with J.F. Champollion, the man who succeeded in deciphering Egyptian hieroglyphics thanks to the "Rosetta

▼ *Chimera of Arezzo*, Etruscan art, 5ᵗʰ cent. B.C.

▼ *Mater Matuta*, Italic goddess of fertility and maternity

Stone". The Antiquarium houses objects of Etruscan art including the *Chimera of Arezzo* (5ᵗʰ century B.C.) the *Arringatore* or Haranguer (1ˢᵗ century B.C.), the *Idolino* (5ᵗʰ century B.C.) and a Hellenistic *head of a horse*. Among the Etruscan cinerary urns particular mention should be made of the fine *Mater Matuta* (5ᵗʰ century B.C.). On the upper floor the collection of Attic ceramics includes the celebrated *François Vase*, a masterpiece of Greek ceramics (6ᵗʰ century B.C.), found in an Etruscan tomb in Chiusi.

Museo di San Marco

The museum building, the Monastery of San Marco, was built by Michelozzo in 1452. Among the famous occupants of the cells were Fra Angelico, Savonarola, and Fra Bartolomeo. The great number of works by Fra Angelico housed here make it particularly important. The entrance to the **Chapter Hall**, frescoed by Fra Angelico with an imposing *Crucifixion*, is in the **Cloister of Sant'Antonino**, also decorated with frescoes (including *St. Dominic at the foot of the Cross*). The **Ospizio dei Pellegrini** or Pilgrims Hostel houses an exceptional series of panel paintings by Fra Angelico: the *Linaioli Altarpiece*, the late *Bosco ai Frati Altarpiece*, the *St. Mark Altarpiece*, the remarkable *Last Judgment*, and

▼ The Cloister of Sant'Antonino, by Michelozzo

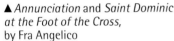
▲ *Annunciation* and *Saint Dominic at the Foot of the Cross,* by Fra Angelico

smaller panels with *Scenes from the life of Christ,* in particular the *Nativity* and *Flight into Egypt.* The most striking in the room, however, is the *Deposition,* acclaimed as Fra Angelico's masterpiece (c. 1435). Upstairs are the austere monks' cells, decorated between 1439 and 1445 with splendid frescoes by Fra Angelico and his helpers. The two pictures of the *Annunciation,* the *Noli me tangere,* the *Crowning with Thorns,* the *Crowning of the Virgin* and the *Transfiguration* are exceptionally fine. The artist's exquisite, almost calligraphic style is simplified, partly for technical reasons, in his frescoes, particularly in the *Annunciation.* The details are reduced to a minimum, and clear pink and alabaster tones predominate. Framed by the architecture of Michelozzo, the heralding angel and the Virgin are imbued with a simplicity and clarity without precedent.

▶ *Last Judgment,* by Fra Angelico

Accademia Gallery

▼ Two striking views
of Michelangelo's *David*

Established in 1784, the Accademia Gallery features 13ᵗʰ-16ᵗʰ century Florentine school paintings and some of Michelangelo's most famous sculptures. The main exhibition halls, the **Salone** and **Tribuna** (above) designed by Emilio De Fabris in the late 1800s, host some of the most extraordinary examples of Michelangelo's sculpture. The four *Prisons* or *Slaves*, roughly blocked out master-

▼ *Saint Matthew*, by Michelangelo

pieces of enormous vigor, were meant for Pope Julius' tomb in Rome (c. 1518). The *St. Matthew* (c. 1505), is the only one of the planned group of apostles ever carved for the Cathedral of Florence, and the *Palestrina*

▲ The *"Bearded" Prison*,
by Michelangelo

▼ *Venus and Cupid* (det.),
by Pontormo

Pietà, a dramatic example of the master's late style, was sculpted for the chapel of Palazzo Barberini in Palestrina. At the end of the Tribuna stands the *David*, an early work of exceptional effect that needs no introduction. It was commissioned by the Republic of Florence as the symbol of Florentine freedom and set in front of Palazzo Vecchio, the city's civic center, in 1504. From a frontal position, the *David* seems almost relaxed, with the weight on his right leg, despite the splendid prominence given to the anatomical features and the dynamic tension visible in every part. In the right hand and arm, in the ribs and the abdomen, Michelangelo achieved a level of realism never seen before. In the face (one must move to the right arm of the tribune to see it) there is a combination of pride and moral strength. The forehead and mouth express unyielding determination, and the eyes seem to burn with an inner fire. The *David* was created at the time of Amerigo Vespucci, Machiavelli, Leonardo da Vinci, Raphael, etc. The statue thus represents more than just David, more than Apollo or even Hercules: in the end it is Michelangelo's monument glorifying Renaissance man. Paintings of the 13th-16th century are to be found in the other rooms of the gallery. Leaving the Academy, we find the Conservatorio Musicale Luigi Cherubini, to our left, at Piazza Belle Arti 2. It was founded in 1809 and enlarged under the Lorraine grand duchy. It houses manuscripts by Rossini, Cherubini, Scarlatti, among others, as well as musical instruments by Stradivari, Amati, and others.

▼ *The Tree of Life*,
by Pacino di Buonaguida

▼ The *Palestrina Pietà*, by Michelangelo

Bargello National Museum

▼The Palazzo del Bargello in a picture of the times and the courtyard with the staircase by Neri di Fioravante

The forbidding palazzo of the Bargello was built in 1255 as headquarters for the Capitano del Popolo. It next became the residence of the Podestà, a kind of governor, and in the 16th century, of the chief of police, the "Bargello". The tall crenellated tower, with bifores and monofores on the sides, is known as the **Volognana**. Since 1859 the rooms have housed the **Museo Nazionale,** one of the most important in the world with its collection of minor arts, arms, Tuscan 15th and 16th century sculpture and della Robbia terracottas. The courtyard on the ground floor is particularly fascinating with the play of arches, the staircase, the many coats of arms on the

◀ *Bacchus*, by Michelangelo

walls and the prevalently 16th century sculptures under the portico. Entrance from the courtyard is to the **Salone del Cinquecento**, with such famous pieces as the *Pitti Tondo*, the *bust of Brutus*, the *Drunken Bacchus,* and *Apollo-David,* all masterpieces by Michelangelo, as well as works by Cellini, Sansovino, Ammannati, and Giambologna. A flight of stairs from the courtyard leads to the upper floor with the **Cappella del Podestà**, with frescoes attributed to Giotto (the portrait of Dante can be seen on the back wall in the scene of *Paradise*). The vast Hall

▲ *Lady with a bouquet of flowers,* by Verrocchio

► *Cosimo I dei Medici*, by Benvenuto Cellini

▲ *Madonna and Child and the Young Saint John*, by Michelangelo, known as the "Pitti Tondo"

houses masterpieces such as Donatello's *David*, the *Young St. John* and the *St. George*, the two reliefs of the *Sacrifice of Isaac* by Ghiberti and Brunelleschi and works by Luca della Robbia. Giovanni and Andrea della Robbia's glazed terracotta production (15th-16th century) is documented on the top floor. One room is devoted to small bronzes and one to an interesting collection of weapons and suits of armor. The **Sala del Verrocchio** contains works by the Florentine master such as the *David* and the bust of a *Lady with a bouquet of flowers*.

▼ Left to right: *Mercury*, by Cellini; *David*, by Donatello; *David*, by Verrocchio

Santa Croce

This magnificent Franciscan Gothic church was begun around the mid-1200s (according to tradition by Arnolfo di Cambio), although it was not consecrated until 1443. Italy's Westminster Abbey, it vaunts Giotto's remarkable frescoes, as well as the tombs of famous Italians. The facade, in 19th century Neo-Gothic style, has a *sagrato* on one side with the *monument to Dante* (1865). In keeping with the Franciscan tradition, the interior is simple and stately although the walls are decorated by numerous tombs and monuments, including Vasari's *tomb of Michelangelo*, Canova's *monument to Vittorio Alfieri,* the *monument to Niccolò Machiavelli,* as well as the *tombs of the composer Rossini, the poet Ugo Foscolo* (right aisle), *Galileo,* and *Ghiberti* (left aisle). On the third right pier is a pulpit by Benedetto da Maiano; on the right wall is a striking *Annunciation* by Donatello. In the right transept are the **Castellani Chapel** and the **Baroncelli Chapel**, with interesting 14th century frescoes. The **Rinuccini Chapel**, with frescoes by Giovanni da Milano is

▼ The facade of Santa Croce and the *monument to Dante* by Enrico Pazzi located on the *sagrato* of the church

◄The Baroncelli Chapel,
frescoed by Taddeo Gaddi

▼ *Funeral monument for Michelangelo,*
designed by Vasari

in the fine 14th century sacristy.
The chapels at the east end of particular note are the **Peruzzi Chapel**
and the **Bardi Chapel**, both with
frescoes by Giotto (*Stories of Saint*

▼The Chiostro Maggiore,
entrance to the Pazzi Chapel

▶ *The Death of Saint Francis,*
by Giotto in the Bardi Chapel

Francis in the **Bardi Chapel**), the **Cappella Maggiore**, with frescoes by Agnolo Gaddi and a wooden *Crucifix* by the Figline Master, and (last on the left) the **Cappella Bardi di Vernio** frescoed by Maso di Banco. On the right side of the church is a large cloister with (at the back) the **Pazzi Chapel**, by Brunelleschi (begun 1443). The *Museo dell'Opera di Santa Croce* is in the old part of the Convent once used as a refectory. It includes works by Taddeo Gaddi, Orcagna, Donatello, Domenico Veneziano, Tino di Camaino and others. In the first room is the great *Crucifix* by Cimabue, so tragically damaged in the flood of 1966 and restored as much as possible.

▲ *Last Judgment* (det.), by Andrea Orcagna in the Museo dell'Opera di Santa Croce

▶ The Monument to Michelangelo, with the bronze copy of the *David* at the center of the square

▼ Piazzale Michelangelo at dusk

Piazzale Michelangelo

With the whole city spread out below your feet, you see, from left to right; the park of the Cascine, the dome and vast bulk of the Cathedral surrounded by the towers and bell towers of medieval Florence, with the Arno in the foreground and its bridges and the cluster of Florentine hills in the background. In the center of the square is a copy of Michelangelo's *David*.

San Miniato al Monte

This superb Romanesque church was built between the 11th and 12th centuries. A 13th century mosaic is above the central window. Inside is the splendid **Cappella del Crocifisso**, designed by Michelozzo in 1448. The crypt is decorated with frescoes by Taddeo Gaddi while there is a large 13th century mosaic in the sanctuary.

Fiesole

This small Etruscan city, so old that its origins are lost in time, stands between two hills to the north of Florence. Its magnificent position, from which the entire valley of the Arno can be seen, its works of art and excavations revealing Etruscan and Roman ruins make it a must for many visitors. The spacious **Piazza Mino da Fiesole** stands at the center of the town. Around it are the 17th century **Seminary**, the **Bishop's Palace** founded in the 11th century and opposite which is the **Cathedral** (dedicated to Saint Romolus), also 11th century. The other buildings on the square are the 14th century **Palazzo Pretorio**, renovated in later times,

decorated with the coats of arms of the Podestà and now Town Hall, with the small 10th century **church of Santa Maria Primerana**, renovated in the 16th century, next to it. In the *Museo Bandini* (behind the apse of the cathedral) are works by Taddeo and Agnolo Gaddi, Lorenzo Monaco, Jacopo del Sellaio as well as Della Robbia terracottas. Opposite it is the entrance to the archaeological area and the *Museo Civico*. At the center of the area is the **Roman theatre**, discovered in 1809 during excavations of the ancient part of Fiesole undertaken in that year by the German baron Friedman von Schellersheim, goes back to the time of Silla (1st century B.C.), and was built in the manner of the Greek theatres. There is a fine view of the hills from the tiers of seats.

▲▼ San Miniato al Monte - The splendid church on the hill known as "Monte alle Croci", behind Piazzale Michelangelo and detail of the apse mosaic

◀▲ Fiesole - Piazza Mino da Fiesole and the facade of the Cathedral

Venice "Bride of the sea"

Venice is universally acclaimed as one of the world's most beautiful cities. It is certainly one of the most unusual both in its history, its appearance, and its urban plan. Venice rises from the water and the first impression is that water is everywhere. Actually, however, the houses and churches are built on hundreds of islets and firmly reinforced by thousands of pylons sunk into the ground. The canals (rii) that separate the islets and where all kinds of boats go up and down are the equivalent of mainland town streets. Some of the islands in the lagoon were already inhabited by fishermen in Roman times, but not until the Middle Ages did it become a clearly defined political and social entity, when it came under the Byzantine sphere of influence, as opposed to the mainland cities that were dominated by the Longobards. In the 9th century, when most of Italy was under Frankish control, Venice embarked on a new form of government, i.e. a duchy headed by a duke (Doge, in Venetian dialect) and backed by the local nobility. Having severed all ties with the Empire of the East, she enjoyed long centuries of prosperity and glory: the Serenissima emerged as a leader in sea trade (especially with the Orient) and with an extraordinary development in the arts. She never went through a feudal period, nor did she exist as a city-state. Rather, the Venetian form of government was that of an aristocratic republic, with a Doge elected and assisted by collegial organisms. The great wealth amassed thanks to the business acumen of the Venetian traders (among them Marco Polo), was a prime factor in sparking-off a great building boom with elegant palaces and countless churches and convents. Venice reached the height of her political and economic power during the 15th and 16th centuries. She extended her dominions on the mainland and successfully fought the Turks. At the same time, Venetian art was thoroughly revolutionizing Italian painting: the

Bellinis, Carpaccio, Giorgione, Titian, Tintoretto, and Veronese were active during these years. Then, in the 17th and 18th centuries, as Venice found herself crushed by the new European powers, decline, both economic and political, began to set in. In 1797 she was annexed by Austria; in 1866 she became part of the Kingdom of Italy. Thenceforth the history of Venice has merged with the history of Italy. This exceptional history has left its mark on the face of the city, a varied, composite face, characterized by elegant monuments, but also by small modest calli, silent rii along which the gondolas slide, taverns, small markets, popular holidays, elegant cafes, theater and cultural events. Venice can be reached by car, by train and by air as well as by sea. The car park in Piazzale Roma can be reached by crossing the Ponte della Libertà, a bridge built next to the railroad bridge in 1933. This great car park is also the point of departure for the buses that connect Venice with its sister cities on the mainland. It takes thirty minutes to get by vaporetto from the Fondamenta di Santa Croce to Piazza San Marco, along the Grand Canal. The trip can also be via motorboat or gondola. The functional modern railroad station was built in 1954. A long bridge inaugurated in 1846 and for which seventy-five thousand pylons were anchored in the lagoon takes one from the mainland to the station of Santa Lucia, named after a pre-existing church dedicated to this saint in the 16th century. Leaving the station we are right at the beginning of the Grand Canal where a vaporetto or a gondola will take you to the heart of the city, by way of its main thoroughfare lined with the splendid residences of old Venetian nobility. The vaporetto is in a sense what the bus or tram are for a normal city. The first examples came to Venice from France in 1881. Ever since, the vaporetti go back and forth regularly every day and have become part of the city landscape.

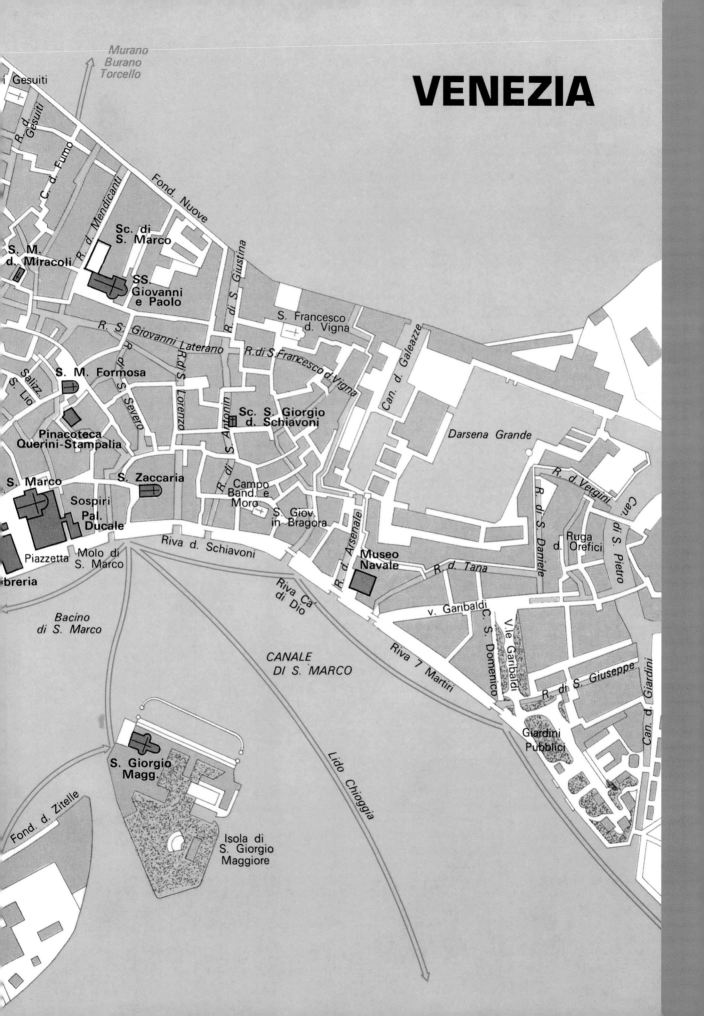

VENEZIA

Murano
Burano
Torcello

i Gesuiti

R. d. Gesuiti

C. d. Fumo

Fond Nuove

R. d. Mendicanti

Sc. di
S. Marco

S. M.
d. Miracoli

SS.
Giovanni
e Paolo

R. di S. Giustina

S. Francesco
d. Vigna

R. S. Giovanni Laterano

R. di S. Francesco d. Vigna

Can. d. Galeazze

S. M. Formosa

R. di S. Lorenzo

R. d. S. Severo

Salizz.
S. Lio

Pinacoteca
Querini-Stampalia

R. di S. Antonin

Sc. S. Giorgio
d. Schiavoni

Darsena Grande

R. d Vergini

R. di S. Pietro

S. Marco

S. Zaccaria

Campo
Band. e
Moro

S. Giov.
in Bragora

R. d. S. Daniele

Ruga
d. Orefici

Can. di S. Pietro

Sospiri
Pal.
Ducale

R. d. Arsenale

Museo
Navale

R. d. Tana

Piazzetta

Molo di
S. Marco

Riva d. Schiavoni

v. Garibaldi

breria

Riva Ca'
di Dio

Riva 7 Martiri

C. S. Domenico

V.le Garibaldi

R. di S. Giuseppe

Can. d. Giardini

Bacino
di S. Marco

CANALE
DI S. MARCO

Giardini
Pubblici

S. Giorgio
Magg.

Lido Chioggia

Fond. d. Zitelle

Isola di
S. Giorgio
Maggiore

Grand Canal

▲ The Grand Canal

Venice's major waterway, the Grand Canal, bisects the whole city. Running from the railway station to San Marco (approximately 1.5 kilometers as the crow flies), it is shaped like an upside down "S". Its vital statistics are: almost 4 kilometers long, maximum depth 5 meters, and average breadth 50 meters. Heavily trafficked by *vaporetti*, gondolas, and craft of every size and shape, the canal is a unique sight, its banks lined with an incredible parade of splendid palaces and churches. The Baroque **Church of the Scalzi** stands at its beginning, on the left. The bridge that crosses the canal here is the **Ponte degli Scalzi**, built in 1934. A bit further on the left, the **Cannaregio Canal** intersects the Grand Canal. Continuing, on the right is the **Fondaco** **dei Turchi**, once the headquarters and trade center of the Oriental merchants. This 13th century building in Venetian-Byzantine style architecturally recalls the Doge's Palace. It houses the *Museo Civico di Storia Naturale* or Natural History Museum. On the right bank, after the **Church of San Stae**, is the **Palazzo Pesaro**, built by Baldassarre Longhena in the 17th century with a massive rusticated lower floor and two portals. It houses the *Galleria d'Arte Moderna* and the *Museo d'Arte Orientale*. A bit beyond on the left side is the renowned **Ca' d'Oro** with a stunning facade of Gothic marble tracery with interlacing arched windows and a lacy crenellation. It was designed by Bartolomeo Bon and Matteo de' Raverti in the imaginative 15th century

▼ The facade of the Church of the Scalzi

▲ Ponte degli Scalzi

▼ The Fondaco dei Turchi

Venetian style and the facade was once gilded, hence the name. Inside is the *Galleria Franchetti* featuring works by Bellini, Titian, Carpaccio, and Guardi. Beyond the **Rialto Bridge**, on the left bank, are two medieval Venetian-Byzantine style palaces, **Palazzo Loredan** and **Palazzo Farsetti**. A bit farther, on the same side, is **Palazzo Grimani**, a 16th century building by Sanmicheli. On the right, where the canal bends to the left, is the elegant 15th century Gothic facade of **Ca' Foscari**, with three superimposed loggias. Just beyond, on the curve itself, is **Palazzo Rezzonico**, seat of the *Museo del Settecento Veneziano*. Opposite is an 18th century palace, **Palazzo Grassi**, used for important art shows. Leaving the bend, you pass beneath the **Accademia Bridge**, a wooden structure first built in 1930 (but with a metal armature). The *Accademia Museum* is on your right. The **Ca' Grande** or Palazzo Corner is a classic building by Jacopo Tatti known as "Il Sansovino". The name Grande

▼ Palazzo Pesaro

◄ Palazzo Loredan and Palazzo Farsetti

▲ The Ca' d'Oro

◀ Palazzo Rezzonico

▼ Palazzo Corner della Ca' Grande

▲ Detail of the facade
of Ca' Foscari

clearly derives from its monumentality. Today seat of the Prefecture, it was built in 1535 for Jacopo Corner and housed the Austrian representative under the Lombard Venetian kingdom. The last buildings on the right bank are the church of **Santa Maria della Salute** and the **Customs Point** (Punta della Dogana), built in the 17th century, on the site where duties had been levied on merchandise arriving by sea ever since the 15th century. On the left is the **Molo di San Marco**.

Rialto Bridge

▼ The Rialto Bridge and the shrine
with the *Virgin* located at the base

The Rialto is the oldest, the most famous and the loveliest of the three bridges spanning the Grand Canal. Originally made of wood, a picture by Carpaccio in the Academy Galleries illustrates the special mechanism with which it was once equipped that allowed the middle section to be moved whereby even the tallest masted ships could sail through. In the 16th century it was decided to rebuild it in stone. A competition was called, attracting the participation of such well-known architects as Michelangelo and Sansovino. Antonio da Ponte, the winner, completed this undertaking in 1592. The canal at this point is only 28 meters wide. The height of the bridge at the center is 7.5 meters. The two ends rest upon 12,000 wooden pylons sunk into the muddy depths. There are twenty-four picturesque shops on the bridge, separated in the middle by two arches that offer access to two upper floors overlooking the Grand Canal. The magnificent view to be had from here makes it one of the most popular places for photographers, tourists and artists.

Santa Maria della Salute

▼ Bird's eye view
of the Punta della Dogana

▲ The majestic
Church of Santa Maria della Salute,
masterpiece by Longhena

The senate of the Republic of Venice decreed that it be built in 1630, a sign of thanksgiving for the end of a plague. Work was entrusted to Longhena but encountered great difficulties due to the subsiding of the land and the supporting walls. The imaginative "curls" supporting the drum were invented by the architect to solve problems of statics. The imposing church is octagonal in plan, with two domes and a facade on the Grand Canal. The spacious interior consists of a circular area surrounded by columns. The side altars are adorned with paintings by Titian, Morlaiter and Luca Giordano. The magnificent high altar was designed by Longhena and embellished with statues by various artists. Next to it is a fine 16th

▼ Detail of the interior
of Santa Maria della Salute

century paschal candlestick in bronze while behind the altar is a 15th century *Madonna and Child.* The most important works, however, are in the **Sacrestia Grande** (Large Sacristy): at the altar, *St. Mark Enthroned and Saints,* by Titian; a 12th century Byzantine mosaic *Virgin and Child;* three canvases by Titian on the ceiling, and Tintoretto's *Wedding at Cana* on the right wall.

Piazzetta

Until the 16th century the Piazzetta, i.e., the square between the San Marco Quay and Piazza San Marco, was a marketplace for foodstuffs and the scene of public executions. On top of the two monolithic columns in red granite standing in the middle are statues of *St. Todaro* (or Theodore, one of the first patron saints of Venice) and a very old *Lion of St. Mark,* of uncertain provenience. To your left (back to the water) is the *Libreria Marciana,* or *Libreria Sansoviniana* designed in the mid-16th century by Jacopo Sansovino for the rare book collection bequeathed to the city by the 15th century Greek humanist scholar, Cardinal Bessarione. The building repeats the typically Venetian solution of a portico with a loggia above in classical forms. Today the building houses a library: the *Biblioteca Nazionale Marciana* and Venice's *Archaeological Museum* with Greek and Roman sculpture. The right side of the Piazzetta is closed off by the Doge's Palace.

▼ Piazzetta San Marco
with its splendid monuments

Piazza San Marco

◄ The Winged Lion, symbol of Venice set under the crowning of the Clock Tower

Originally, Piazza San Marco was a grass-covered open space traversed by a canal and with a church at each of its shorter ends, San Teodoro and San Geminiano. Subsequent transformation and embellishments made it into one of the most beautiful squares in the world, civic and religious heart of the city. It is an open-air parlor till late at night, with crowds of tourists, the ever-present pigeons, elegant shops, small tables set out in the square and the orchestras of its famous old cafes. The paving with its white bands dates to the 18th century. It is surrounded by the two solemn buildings of the **Procuratie Vecchie** (Old Courts) and the **Procuratie Nuove** (New Courts), the **Napoleonic Wing** (early 1800s)

▼ The Procuratie Vecchie and the Napoleonic Wing

▼ Detail of the Procuratie Vecchie

▼ The Bell Tower of Saint Mark's

▲ The Clock Tower

▼ Sansovino's Loggetta

and, opposite, the **Basilica of San Marco**. The Procuratie Vecchie (like the Nuove built to house the Procuratori of San Marco) dates to the late 15th and early 16th century. The Procuratie Nuove (now housing the *Museo Civico Correr*) was begun by Scamozzi at the end of the 16th century and finished by Longhena in 1640. This unique architectural ensemble is completed by the **Bell Tower**, with the 16th century **Loggetta** with its three arches by Sansovino and the **Clock Tower**, with the bell on which the famous "Moors" strike the hours on a terrace.

▲ Saint Mark's Basilica

St. Mark's Basilica

In 828 the mortal remains of St. Mark the Evangelist were brought to Venice from Alexandria in Egypt. On this occasion it was decided to build a church worthy of containing such a precious relic, and one befitting a burgeoning city anxious to show off its wealth and grandeur. Most of the grandiose basilica was built, bit-by-bit, between the 11th and 15th centuries. The result is a harmonious blend of Byzantine gold, Gothic spires, Romanesque round arches, and Islamic domes, bearing witness to the "interna-

tional" and eclectic vocation of Venice. The facade is horizontal in layout, with two super-posed levels of great arches. The lower level contains the five great portals, separated by Romanesque columns and reliefs, and by the mosaic lunettes, all redone in the Baroque pe-

◄ The famous Horses of St. Mark's

► Moorish decoration and mosaic on the San Alipio portal

▲ The Tetrarchs

▼ Mosaic of the central portal with *Christ in Glory and the Last Judgment*

riod except for the first one on the left, dated 1270, that shows what the basilica looked like at the time. Four of the five arches on the upper level are also decorated with 17th century mosaics and elaborately embellished with sculpture by the Dalle Masegne (14th-15th century). On the terrace separating the two levels are the four famous gilded bronze **Horses** (recently replaced by bronze copies: the originals are in the Basilica Museum) brought to Venice from Constantinople by Doge Enrico Dandolo in 1204. They seem to have been cast in Greece around the 4th century B.C. On the corner of the Basilica (Doge's Palace side) is a porphyry group of the so-called *Tetrarchs,* a 4th century B.C. Syrian work. From the central portal you enter the

Basilica atrium where the vaults and cupolas are decorated with mosaics. The finest are undoubtedly the *scenes from Genesis* (13th-14th centuries). The interior is in the

▲ The Pala d'Oro

◀ Interior of St. Mark's Basilica

▼ The so-called "Genesis" dome with its splendid mosaics

shape of a Greek cross with three aisles to each arm of the cross, and *matronei* (women's galleries) running the length of the upper level. Mosaics cover the walls and the floor (subject: the *lives of Christ* and of *St. Mark*). The Byzantine style gold-ground mosaics were made between the 12th-13th centuries by Venetian craftsmen, while others were made later (those on the inner facade were designed by Tintoretto and others). Even older mosaics (predating the year 1000) are to be found between the apse windows. The great *Christ* looming up in the apse dates from the 16th century. A carved screen separates the nave from the choir. The four-

teen statues adorning it were sculpted in the 14th century by the Dalle Masegnes. On either side are pulpits: the 14th century double pulpit and the so-called "Reliquary Pulpit". The relics of St. Mark are preserved inside the richly decorated high altar. Behind the altar is one of the masterpieces of medieval art, the *Pala d'Oro* (Golden Screen). Made of gold, gemstones, and enamels, it was crafted between the 10th and 14th centuries. The enamel in the center depicts *Christ* with the *Evangelists,* while the *Virgin, Apostles,* and *Prophets* are portrayed in the others. On the right wall of the left transept is a famous Byzantine icon known as the *Madonna Nicopeia* (Victorious Virgin). Dated around the 10th century, it was brought to Venice from Constantinople by the

▼ The *Madonna Nicopeia*

returning Crusaders in 1204. Access to the **Cappella della Madonna dei Màscoli** and the **Cappella di San Isidoro**, both covered with magnificent mosaics, is also from this transept. In the right transept is the

▲ The Cappella di San Isidoro

▲ The *Madonna with Saints Mark and John the Evangelist*, marble triptych over the altar in the Cappella dei Màscoli

entrance to the **Treasury** with a wealth of Byzantine gold work most of which also arrived in Venice with the Crusade of 1204. Access to the 4th century **Baptistery** is from the right aisle. It has a Baptismal Font, designed by Sansovino, and adorned with marbles and mosaics (1545). Returning to the Basilica atrium, go up one flight to the interesting *Museo Marciano* and the outdoor terrace where the horses are displayed.

▼ Detail of the dome of the Baptistery

▲The Doge's Palace
and the bust of Doge S. Venier,
by A. Vittoria, inside

▼ Well curb
in the courtyard of the Palace

Doge's Palace

This extraordinarily elegant and light structure, with the Gothic arches of the ground-floor portico, the airy loggia with Gothic tracery above and the patterned white and pink stonework on the upper floor, was built in the 9th century as the doge's residence. It was frequently renovated by famous architects such as the Dalle Masegnes, Rizzo, and da Ponte and achieved its present aspect in the 16th century. The splendid rooms inside still have their original decoration, furniture, paintings and sculpture. The balconies on the facade are by the Dalle Masegne (on the lagoon side, 1404) and the school of Sansovino (facing the Piazzetta, 1536). Entrance to the Doge's Palace is through the richly ornamented **Porta della Carta** (Door of the Bills), by members of the Bon family (1442). In the courtyard are two 16th century *bronze well curbs*. On the left is the so-called *Foscari Arcade*. The monumental staircase of the adjoining **Cortiletto dei Senatori**, the **Scala dei Giganti** (Giants' Staircase), was designed by Antonio Rizzo in the 1500s. It has been given this name because of the enormous *statues of Mars and Neptune* sculpted by Sansovino. At the top of these stairs the Doge was crowned as soon as he was elected, in the presence of the people and the dignitaries of the Republic. Ambassadors and illustrious guests were also received here. A series of decorated halls, most of them the work of the great 16th century Venetian masters, starts on the second floor. We shall list only the highlights. In the *Sale della Pinacoteca* (Picture Gallery rooms), once the doge's private apartments: *Lion of St. Mark*, by Carpaccio, *Pietà* by Giovanni Bellini, and works by Hieronymus Bosch. On the next floor, the *Sala delle Quattro Porte* (Room

▲ The Porta della Carta

▼ The courtyard of the Doge's Palace

of the Four Doors) with frescoes by Tintoretto and a Titian painting depicting *Doge Antonio Grimani kneeling before Faith*; the **Sala del Collegio** (Room of the College) with a superb ceiling adorned with paintings by Veronese; the **Sala del Senato** (Senate Room) with paintings by Tintoretto (on the ceiling, *Venice, Queen of the Seas); the Sala del Consiglio dei Dieci* (Room of the Council of Ten) with paintings by Veronese. Here, the highly feared magistrates assembled to investigate crimes of a political nature against the security of the State. In the **Sala della Bussola** (Room of the Second Door), named after the double door called the "Bussola", the condemned and accused waited for decisions on their crimes against

▲ The Giants' Staircase

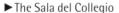
► The Sala del Collegio

▲ The Scala d'Oro

▲ The Sala del Senato

the security of the Republic. In the *Sala d'Armi* (Armory) are exhibited arms and armor of great renown. This collection of 15th and 16th century pieces is truly unique, as it is made up of weapons really used to defend the palace (plus parade and jousting arms). These rooms once served as prisons, but in the early 14th century they were already used as armory. They now house a carefully arranged and interesting collection of arms from past centuries: swords, picks, halberds, harquebusiers, culverins, suit of armor of Henry IV, king of France, two suits of armor that belonged to the Sforza, an harquebus with twenty barrels and a *bronze bust of Francesco Morosini*, by Parodi. The **Scala dei Censori** takes us back to the second floor and the *Sala del Maggior Consiglio* (Hall of the Greater Council) where the supreme Venetian magistrates gathered in council. The room is 54 meters (176 feet) long, 25 meters (82 feet) wide, and 15.40 (51 feet) high. Destroyed by fire in 1557, it was rebuilt by Antonio da Ponte and embellished with paintings whose iconography was suggested by the erudite Florentine Girolamo de' Bardi and the Venetian historian F. Sansovino and it involves the glorification of the Venetian Republic. The huge painting of

▲ The "lion's mouth" used for secret denunciations in the Sala della Bussola

► The Triumphal Arch by A. Tirali in the Sala dello Scrutinio

▲ The Hall of Henry IV

▲ The *Drunkenness of Noah*, carved on the south corner capital of the Doges' Palace

► The entrance to the Prigioni Nuove

Paradise over the tribune is by Tintoretto. A large oval panel on the ceiling, by Paolo Veronese, depicts the *Apotheosis of Venice*, with spectacular scenic effects. The *Sala dello Scrutinio* (Voting Room) was rebuilt by Antonio da Ponte after the fire of 1577. The paintings which celebrate the victories of the Venetian Republic on the high seas were suggested by Girolamo de' Bardi. The **Triumphal Arch** against the far wall was built by A. Tirali in 1694 to honor Admiral Morosini.

Bridge of Sighs

The bridge joins the Doge's Palace to the 16th century Prigioni Nuove (New Prisons) and was designed by Antonio Contini in the decorative 17th century Baroque style. The sighs the bridge was named for actually go back to a 19th century Romantic tradition; they had nothing to do with sighs of love, but were probably the much more tragic exhalations of the condemned as they cast a last glance at Venice through the grille windows along the way. Beyond the **Ponte della Paglia** we continue

▲ The Bridge of Sighs

down the **Riva degli Schiavoni** now a favorite promenade and once the mooring station for trading vessels coming from Schiavonia (now Dalmatia). Lined with cafes and hotels it is the most popular Venetian promenade along the entire basin of San Marco, up to Giardini di Castello in which part of the Biennale d'Arte Moderna is held.

▼ Riva degli Schiavoni

◄ Ponte della Paglia

▶ Bird's eye view
of the Island of San Giorgio

▼ The Church of San Giorgio
Maggiore, designed by Palladio

Island of St. Giorgio

Across from the pier of St. Mark's is the Isle of St. George with the lovely white facade of the **Church of San Giorgio Maggiore**. The church was designed by Palladio in 1565 and the facade employs the typical "giant order" he used in countless other buildings: i.e. four enormous Corinthian columns supporting a huge triangular tympanum surmounted by statues of the Savior and two angels. The elegant luminous interior contains some outstanding Tintorettos such as the *Last Supper* and *Shower of Manna* in the sanctuary and a *Deposition* in the **Cappella dei Morti**. The *Saint George and the Dragon* is by Carpaccio. The adjoining monastery is now occupied by an international renowned art and cultural institution, the Cini Foundation – thanks to which the whole architectural complex was restored.

Accademia Galleries

▼ Entrance to the Accademia

The *Accademia di Pittori e Scultori* was founded in 1750 with headquarters in the Giardinetti of San Marco. Piazzetta, its first director, was succeeded by Tiepolo in 1756. In the late 1700s it was moved to its present location on the Grand Canal in a former monastery, the Convento della Carità. Many prominent artists, including Canova, trained here, although gradually the Accademia

▼ *Saint George*, by Andrea Mantegna

▼ *Madonna and Child*, by Antonio Vivarini

▲ *Pietà*, by Giovanni Bellini

became as much a museum as an art school. The plural *"Gallerie"*, as the museum is called in Italian, is used because originally there were two separate collections, one of plaster casts and one of paintings. Today, it ranks as one of the most important art collections in Italy. The first exhibition hall is primarily devoted to the 14th century Venetian school. Major works include: *Coronation of the Virgin,* by Paolo Veneziano; *Mystic Marriage of St. Catherine* and *Annunciation Altarpiece*, by Lorenzo

▼ *The Tempest*, by Giorgione

◀ *The Feast in the House of Levi,*
by Paolo Veronese

▲ *Portrait of a Gentleman* (det.),
by Lorenzo Lotto

Veneziano; *Madonna della Misericordia* and *Coronation of the Virgin,* by Jacobello del Fiore, Antonio Vivarini's robust 15th cent. *Madonna and Child.* Room II contains paintings by Cima da Conegliano: a *Sacra Conversazione (Madonna and Saints)* and the *Virgin of the Orange Tree* and the *Calling of the Sons of Zebedee* by Marco Basaiti. Room III: *Madonna and Saints*, attributed to Sebastiano del Piombo. Room IV: *St. George*, by Mantegna and *St. Jerome and donor,* by Piero della Francesca. Room V: *Pietà, Madonna degli Alberelli,* and *Allegories,* all by Giovanni Bellini, and Giorgione's masterpiece, the unsettling *Tempest.* Room VI: works by Tintoretto, Bordone and Titian. Room VII: *Portrait of a Gentleman,* by Lotto. Room VIII: works by Palma the Elder. Room X: *Feast in the House of Levi,* a huge canvas by Paolo Veronese, one of the master's most famous works, and the *Miracles of St. Mark* cycle, by Tintoretto. Rooms XI through XV are devoted to Tintoretto, Veronese,

16th century Venetian school, Tiepolo, and 18th century landscapists. Room XVI: four mythological scenes by Tiepolo. Room XVII: *views* by Guardi, Bellotto, and Canaletto, pastel portraits

▼ *Saint Jerome and donor,*
by Piero della Francesca

▲ *Procession of the Relic in Piazza San Marco,* by Gentile Bellini

▼ *The Arrival of the Ambassadors,* by Vittore Carpaccio

by Carriera, and genre scenes by Pietro Longhi including the *Fortune-Teller,* the *Dancing Lesson,* and the *Pharmacist.* Room XVIII: three sculptures by Canova. Room XX: the series of large 15th century paintings depicting the *Miracles of the Relic of the Cross,* and especially: *Miraculous Healing of a Possessed Man,* by Carpaccio, and *Procession in Piazza San Marco,* by Gentile Bellini. Room XXI: Carpaccio's remarkable cycle of the *Story of St. Ursula:* the *Arrival of the Ambassadors, St. Ursula meets Ereus* and the *Burial of St. Ursula.* The following hall is devoted to the 15th century, while the last room, with a remarkable gilded carved ceiling, once the Hostel of the Scuola della Carità, contains outstanding works including Titian's *Presentation of the Virgin,* an imposing composition of 1538.

Santi Giovanni e Paolo

The Venetian "Zanipolo" is none other than the contraction in the local dialect of Giovanni and Paolo, or John and Paul, the saints to whom the church is dedicated. This huge Gothic convent church was begun in 1246 and the facade was left incomplete around the mid-1400s, period in which Bartolomeo Bon added the portal. The 14th century apse area is particularly lovely. The imposing interior with a nave and side aisles contains the tombs of important personages in Venetian history. The most important are the *tombs of Admiral Marcantonio Bragadin* (right aisle, 16th century), *Doge Tommaso Mocenigo*, Tuscan school (15th century, left aisle) and of *Doge Pietro Mocenigo,* by Pietro Lombardo (inner facade, 15th century). Among the other notable

works adorning the building are: the *St. Vincenzo Ferrer Altarpiece,* by Giovanni Bellini (second right-hand altar); *St. Antonino giving Alms,* by Lorenzo Lotto (right transept); and a splendid chapel, the **Cappella del Rosario**, with paintings by Veronese. The statue in the square, to the right of the church, is Andrea del Verrocchio's 1496 masterpiece, the *monument to Bartolomeo Colleoni (Condottiero* of the Republic of Venice).

▲ *Equestrian monument to Bartolomeo Colleoni,* by Andrea Verrocchio

◄ The apse of the Church of San Zanipolo

►The *Assumption*, by Titian

Santa Maria Gloriosa dei Frari

Also known as **Santa Maria Assunta**, the Church of the Friars on the Campo of Santa Maria Gloriosa dei Frari is one of Venice's most important monuments. Like San Zanipolo, it contains the tombs of great Venetians. Begun by the Franciscan monks around 1250 – some claim after a design by Nicola Pisano - it was re-elaborated and enlarged by Scipione Bon in 1338 and not finished until 1443. The stark Romanesque-Gothic facade is divided into three sections by pilasters with pinnacles at the top. Over the portal is a statue of *Christ Resurrected* by Alessandro Vittoria, flanked by two figures attributed to the school of the Bon family. The Romanesque bell tower is one of the tallest in Venice after that of San Marco. It was built at the end of the 14th century. The Latin-cross interior with a nave separated from the aisles by 12 columns is imposing and simple, in conformity to the Franciscan spirit. Among the *monuments dedicated to illustrious Venetians* between the 14th and 18th century mention must be made of the one to *Titian* (right aisle), erected in the 1800s on the site where the painter was traditionally thought to be buried, the *monument to Canova* (left aisle), designed by the master himself, and the *monument to Doge Niccolò Tron* (apse), by Antonio Rizzo (15th century). Exceptional works of art complete the decoration of the church: Titian's famous altarpiece of the *Assumption* (1518) behind the high altar; Titian's *Madonna di Ca' Pesaro* (1526) in the left aisle, the altarpiece with *Saint Ambrose and Saints* by Alvise Vivarini and Marco Basaiti in the Cappella dei Milanesi and the triptych with the *Madonna Enthroned and Saints* by Giovanni Bellini in the sacristy. Moving along the left flank of the church of the Frari one reaches **Campo San Rocco**.

▼The facade of the Church of Santa Maria Gloriosa dei Frari

San Rocco

Dominating the triangular-shaped Campo San Rocco, is the 16th century *Scuola Grande di San Rocco* (School of St. Roch). The decision to construct this complex and dedicate it to the plague saint, Roch, was taken in 1515 after a terrible epidemic. Of all the Venetian *scuole,* it is by far the most important one – if only for the number and quality of its Tintorettos. The great artist was commissioned to decorate the so-called Sala dell'Albergaria after a competition in which Paolo Veronese, Zuccari, and other equally famous artists took part. At the center of the ceiling of the **Sala dell'Albergaria** (on the upper floor) is Tintoretto's winning competition entry, St. Roch in glory. The great artist was engaged on the project from 1563 to 1588, painting epi-

▲ Campo San Rocco

sodes from the life of Christ, including a magnificent *Crucifixion*, on the walls. In the rectangular *Salone Maggiore* (Great Hall), we find a self-portrait of the artist aged 66 by one of the doors. On the ceiling are *21 Old Testament scenes,* also by Tintoretto. To the left of the al-

▲ *Allegory of the School of San Teodoro,* by Tintoretto

▼ ▶ *Last Supper* and *Christ before Pilate,* by Tintoretto

▲ ▶ Details of the *Crucifixion* by Tintoretto

▼ The facade of the Church of San Rocco

tar is an *Annunciation* by Titian, while along the walls there are *Scenes from the life of Christ.* In the nearby ***Sala della Cancelleria*** (Chancery Room) the *Ecce Homo* has been attributed to Titian. Downstairs, we enter the grandiose ***Salone Terreno*** or ground floor room divided by two rows of Corinthian pillars, also decorated by Tintoretto. The **Church of San Rocco**, originally a Renaissance building, was rebuilt in the 18th century by Giovanni Scalfarotto. The facade was inspired by the graceful front of the Scuola. Inside the single-aisled church with a dome over the sanctuary are several works by Tintoretto: the *Annunciation* (to the right of the organ), *St. Roch before the Pope* (on the left), and *St. Roch in the Desert* (first altar on the right). There are also several fine paintings portraying *Scenes from the life of St. Roch* along the sanctuary walls. An urn by the main altar contains the relics of the Saint.

HIGH WATER

*Venice is built upon a forest of piles anchored into the lagoon to reinforce the islets on which the buildings stand. The sea, which has always supported the city's economic and political well-being, has often represented danger as well. Sudden tides and sea-storms have time and again threatened the fragile city – nobody will ever forget the **high tide of November 1966** that at first made it seem as though the city would never survive. The phenomenon of high tides (called "acqua alta" or high*

water in Venetian) is such a common experience that the Venetian have come to accept it philosophically, without making too much fuss. The water seems to have a special fondness for Piazza San Marco and the Basilica, where it can get more than half a meter deep so that one sometimes sees gondolas on the square, or even beneath the arcades. A wooden gangway for pedestrian traffic is always on hand when necessary.

Lido of Venice

With its splendid beach and luxurious hotels, the Isola del Lido is thought of as the high society and seaside appendix of Venice to which it is connected by vaporetti. In the 1800s it was popular with artists and poets such as Shelley and Byron. Thomas Mann made it famous with his splendid novel "Death in Venice" which was made into a film later by Luchino Visconti, world famous cinema director. With its luxurious shops, **Viale Santa Maria Elisabetta** is the focal point of the jet set. The greatest tourist attraction however is the international *Venice Film Festival,* held in the **Palazzo del Cinema**. Since 1932, the festival has been bringing famous stars and directors to the Lido in the period between August and September.

▼ Lido di Venezia

Murano

In antiquity it was known as Amurianum. The populations of Altino and other ancient centers on the mainland sought asylum there from the threat of the Huns. Murano soon achieved an enviable condition of well-being. Around the 10th-11th centuries it became one of the major lagoon centers. The tradition of *glass-blowing,* still the basis of the city's great renown, dates back to that period, although it received its greatest boost in the 13th century. A visit to Murano must include first and foremost a walk along the characteristic **Canale degli Angeli** and the **Rio dei Vetrai**. The *Glass Museum* is on the Canale di San Donato. Splendid examples of Murano production of various periods are on exhibit, including the famous 15th century *Barovier cup,* and outstanding examples of foreign production. Next to the museum is the **Church of Santi Maria e Donato,** a Ravennate-style church with a richly ornamented 12th century apse and a square bell tower. The highlights of the striking interior include frescoes and the floor mosaics. The 15th century church of **San Pietro Martire** on Rio dei Vetrai contains paintings by Tintoretto, Giovanni Bellini and Veronese.

become an important bishopric. Torcello's decline was a result of the overpowering competition from Venice and malaria. All that remains now of the entire urban complex to bear witness to its glorious past are the solemn, extraordinary buildings on its grassy square, surrounded by green vegetable gardens. The **Cathedral** dedicated to **Santa Maria Assunta** was founded in the 7th century and rebuilt in the 11th in Ravennate style. Next to it is the majestic tall bell tower (11th century). The inner facade bears an imposing mosaic *Last Judgment* in pure Byzantine style (12th century). The apse conch bears a mosaic of the *Virgin and Child* dating to the 13th century. Other mosaics, sarcophaguses and reliefs complete the decoration. Next to the cathedral is **Santa Fosca**, a 10th-11th century central plan building, surrounded by a porch. The Greek cross interior is of considerable architectural interest. Opposite Santa Fosca, in the square, is the so-called *caregon*, an old marble seat traditionally indicated as "Attila's Throne". The other two buildings on the grassy square are the **Palazzo dell'Archivio** and the **Palazzo del Consiglio**, now housing the *Museo dell'Estuario* with archaeological material from various centers of the lagoon.

▲▼ Torcello – Cathedral of Santa Maria Assunta and Church of Santa Fosca

▲▼ Murano – The apse of the Church of Ss. Maria e Donato and bird's eye view

Torcello

This silent little island, today practically uninhabited, was once a mighty urban center and Venice's major rival. It was founded in 452 by refugees from the mainland city of Altino and by the 7th century had

Naples "City of a thousand faces"

With its mild climate, art and architecture, beautiful setting, excellent cuisine and picturesque nooks and crannies, Naples is unquestionably one of the loveliest of Italian cities. It was founded by the Greeks around the 7th century B.C. as Parthenope (after a mythical siren), and the name was later changed to Neapolis (New Town). In Roman times it was famed as a vacation site, although it remained a highly cultured Greek city in appearance and customs, with more than its share of theaters. Nero and Lucullus were among the famous men who lived there, as well as Virgil who is also buried there. In the 6th century it fell under Byzantine rule where it remained (formally at least for it was actually fully autonomous) until 1139, when it became part of the Norman kingdom. In the Middle Ages it ranked as the most important of the Campanian cities and the history of the region and that of Naples were in a sense one and the same. The Swabian Hohenstauffen dynasty (13th century) succeeded the Normans and with Frederick II the city became an important center of art and cul-

ture. Between the late 13th and 14th century under the House of Anjou its standing increased. It was then that the Maschio and Castel Sant'Elmo were built and outstanding artists such as Simone Martini, Pietro Cavallini and Tino di Camaino, as well as famous writers such as Boccaccio, were drawn to Naples. In the 15th century power passed to the House of Aragon and in the 16th century the Spanish troops arrived and the Kingdom of Naples was ruled by Spanish viceroys. Culturally and economically the period of prosperity lasted till the early 17th century. The aborted popular revolt led by Masaniello dates to 1647. In 1656 the plague killed over 400,000 Neapolitans. The Bourbons became the new arbiters in the 18th century and cultural and artistic activity blossomed with the construction of the Capodimonte Palace and the adjacent porcelain factory whose products soon became famous throughout Europe, with the music of Cimarosa and Pergolesi, and the philosophical thought of Giovan Battista Vico. Then in the 19th century the brief period of Napoleonic rule was followed by the reign of Murat and

the restoration of the Bourbons. In 1860 Garibaldi arrived and Naples was annexed to the Kingdom of Italy. Recent history includes philosophers like Croce, the theater, both in dialect and in Italian, from Scarpetta to the De Filippo family, and the four heroic days during which Naples was liberated from the enemy occupation of 1943.

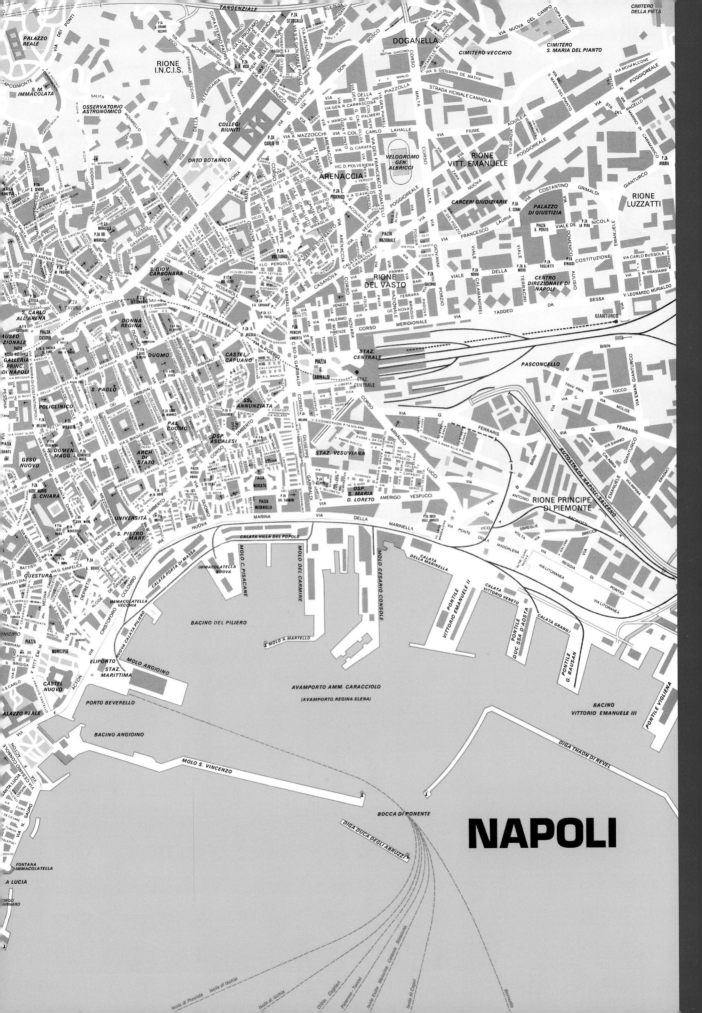

NAPOLI

The Gulf of Naples

I t is hard to know where to look in this lovely gulf with its unique views, where sky and sea merge on the horizon and with Mergellina, Posillipo, Marechiaro, the island of Nisida. The visitor leaving Naples is haunted by a sense of wistfulness and promises in his heart to return.

Cathedral

B uilt in the 13th century and subsequently transformed, the facade, except for the three Gothic portals (1407) decorated with reliefs by Antonio Baboccio, dates to the 19th century. Inside, entrance to the **Chapel of San Gennaro** or **Treasury**, is in the right aisle. This Baroque masterpiece dates to the early 1600s and was frescoed by Domenichino and Lanfranco. It contains the famous relics of the blood of Saint Gennaro (Januarius), patron saint of the city. In May and September crowds gather to witness the miraculous liquefaction of the blood contained in the two phials. A chapel in the transept contains an *Assumption* by Perugino. The **Cappella Minutolo** and the underground **Cappella Carafa** with the 16th century *statue of Cardinal Carafa in prayer* are also of interest. In the left hand aisle is what remains of the **early Christian Basilica of Santa Restituta**, and the **Baptistery** with 5th century mosaics.

▲ The nineteenth century facade of the Cathedral of San Gennaro

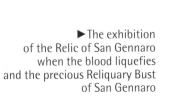
► The exhibition of the Relic of San Gennaro when the blood liquefies and the precious Reliquary Bust of San Gennaro

San Lorenzo Maggiore

Built by the Franciscans between the 13th and 14th century, this is one of the loveliest of Neapolitan Gothic churches. It was here that Boccaccio met Fiammetta (his muse) in 1334. Petrarch lived here in 1345, in the annexed convent. The interior has a nave only, with side chapels. Among the works of art are a 14th century wooden *Crucifix*, the *tomb of Catherine of Austria* by Tino di Camaino (c. 1325), the *tomb of Robert of Artois and Joan of Durazzo* (1399). The cloister (18th century) and the remains of Greek and Roman buildings can be reached from the church.

▶ The facade of San Lorenzo Maggiore

▼ Piazza del Municipio
in front of the Stazione Marittima of Naples, on the right the Maschio Angioino and in the background, Mt. Vesuvius

Maschio Angioino

Known also as **Castel Nuovo**, the dungeon was built by the Angevins around 1280. Restored in the early 1900s, it now looks as it did after the Aragonese modifications of the 15th century. It was the seat first of the Court of Anjou, then of the Aragonese court and finally of the Spanish viceroy. The entrance to this massive castle with its large cylindrical towers consists of the majestic **Triumphal Arch** built for Alfonso I (1443) and decorated by sculptors from varying places. Of interest inside is the **Palatine Chapel** or **of Santa Barbara** and the **Hall of Barons**. Fourteenth-century frescoes as well as works by Mattia Preti, Solimena, Vincenzo Gemito and Caracciolo are in the *Museo Civico* of Castel Nuovo. Guglielmo Monaco's finely sculpted *bronze door* of around 1475 is also in this museum. A cannon ball is embedded in the lower left panel.

▼View of the Maschio Angioino and detail of the lovely Triumphal Arch

Galleria Umberto 1

This impressive and elegant gallery, with its daring glass and wrought-iron roof and its typical belle époque aspect, dates to the end of the 19th century. At the time galleries of this type were being built in various other Italian cities. Famous personages such as D'Annunzio, Salvatore di Giacomo, Scarfoglio, etc. used to meet here in the **Teatro Margherita**.

▲ Galleria Umberto I and a detail of the glass and iron covering

▲ View of Piazza Plebiscito, with the Basilica of San Francesco di Paola, flanked by the hemicycle portico

▼ Palazzo Reale at night

Palazzo Reale

Begun in 1602 by Domenico Fontana for the viceroy's court, Joachim Murat later also stayed in the palace. The broad porticoed facade overlooks **Piazza Plebiscito**. The **Grand Staircase** leads to the **State Apartments**, with elegantly decorated rooms, furniture, 17th and 18th century paintings of Neapolitan school, furnishings and tapestries. Of interest is the **Court Theater** (1768) by Ferdinando Fuga. The building is also the seat of the *National Library* and contains, among others, a collection of papyri from Herculaneum.

▲ Rear part of the Palazzo Reale

▼ The Monumental Staircase leading to the Historical Apartments

▲▼ Two lovely rooms in the Palazzo Reale

Castel dell'Ovo

The castle stands on the picturesque rocky islet of **Borgo Marinaro**, with its old fishermen's houses and famous restaurants overlooking the small **port of Santa Lucia**. It was built in the 12th century over a Basilian monastery that stood on the site of the Roman villa of Lucullus. The name derives from a medieval legend according to which Virgil (thought at the time to have been a magician) had hidden a magic egg (*ovo*) here, with catastrophic results were it to be broken. The massive walls enclose towers, dungeons, Gothic halls and a few cells from the old convent.

▼◀The picturesque port of Santa Lucia and a plaque with an "ode" dedicated to the small port

▲ The massive Castel dell'Ovo,
where exhibitions
and meetings are now also held

◄ The Borgo Marinaro
with the massive Castel dell'Ovo

► Remains of the Roman villa
of Lucius Licinius Lucullus,
the original nucleus
of Castel dell'Ovo

Castel S. Elmo

This is one of the keys for a historical understanding of Parthenope, for from its imposing bastions an eye could be kept on what was happening in the city below and any enemies who might appear on the horizon. The strategic site appealed to the Angevins who built the fort in the first half of the 14th century. The present star-shaped plan dates to modifications carried out for the Aragonese by the Viceroy Pedro of Toledo. For some time, the castle, initially known as **Belforte**, was a military prison but has now been given over to civil use. It contains the **Church of S. Elmo** (16th cent.) and the 17th century **Chapel of S.** **Maria del Pilar**. The castle drill grounds offer one of the finest panoramas around.

▲ A view of the castle that shows the long straight street known as "Spaccanapoli"

▼ General view of Castel S. Elmo and of the Certosa di San Martino

▲The Certosa di San Martino
that dominates the city
from the hill of the Vomero

Certosa di San Martino

▼The lovely Great Cloister
of the Certosa di San Martino

The monastery dominates the city from the Vomero hill, in a splendid panoramic position. It was built in the 14th century by Tino di Camaino and other architects, commissioned by the House of Anjou, and then remodeled in the 17th century by Cosimo Fanzago in Baroque

style. It is now the premises of the **Museo Nazionale di San Martino**. The 16th century church, by Dosio and Fanzago, is splendidly decorated with marbles, sculptures and 17th century paintings of Neapolitan school. These include a *Deposition* by Massimo Stanzione, Ribera's *Prophets*, *The Washing of the Feet* by Battistello Caracciolo, works by Vaccaro, Reni and Solimena. There is a fresco by Luca Giordano in the **Treasury Chapel**. The Museum also contains the collection of 18th century ***Nativity Scenes*** or ***Christmas Cribs***, one of the most interesting and characteristic expressions of Neapolitan art; the ***Picture Gallery*** with works by Solimena, Salvator Rosa, Caracciolo, Luca Giordano and 19th century Neapolitan artists; the ***Sculpture Section***, with works by Tino di Camaino, Sammartino and Pietro Bernini; the ***Minor Arts Section***, with Murano glass and Capodimonte porcelains. The **Great Cloister** of the convent (16th-17th century) is magnificent.

▼The well in the Chiostro di San Martino

▼Panorama of the Certosa di San Martino

▲ Apse end
of San Domenico Maggiore

San Domenico Maggiore

Built in the 13th and 14th centuries, San Domenico is a good example of Angevin Gothic architecture, despite various renovations. The church apse gives onto the square of the same name, with, at the center, the Baroque votive monument known as **Guglia di San Domenico** or St. Dominic's spire, built in 1658 to mark the end of an epidemic of the plague. Inside, in the **Cappellone del Crocifisso**, with a frescoed vault, is a 13th century *Crucifix,* said to have spoken to Saint Thomas of Aquinas. There is a fresco by Solimena (1709) in the sacristy as well as works by Luca Giordano and the school of Tino di Camaino.

▲▶ The Baroque Guglia
di San Domenico and the interior
of the Church of San Domenico

Cappella Sansevero

Built between 1590 and the middle of the 18th century by the Sangro family, the chapel is decorated with magnificent sculptures: *Disillusion* by Francesco Queirolo, *Modesty* by Antonio Corradini and the *Veiled Christ* by Giuseppe Sammartino. A room nearby contains two macabre but interesting examples of experiments in the mummification of cadavers carried out by one of the princes of Sangro.

▶ *Modesty*, by Antonio Corradini

▼ The *Veiled Christ*, by Giuseppe Sammartino

Archaeological Museum
(Museo Archeologico Nazionale)

▼ The premises of the Museo Archeologico Nazionale

With its rich documentation of Greco-Roman art and countless finds from Pompeii, Herculaneum and Stabiae this is one of the largest and most important archaeological museums in the world. Founded in the 18th century by the Bourbons, the premises are in a large 16th century palazzo, formerly a barracks and subsequently University premises. On the museum ground floor are the *Marble Sculptures:* among those of note, the famous group of *Tyrannicides*, Roman copy of the Greek

▲ *Aphrodite Sosandra*, from Stabiae

◄ *Hercules and Telephus*, from Herculaneum

▲ *Battle of Darius and Alexander,*
Pompeian mosaic

▶ *Ephebus,*
from Pompeii

original by Kritios and Nesiotes (5ᵗʰ cent. B.C.); the relief with *Hermes, Orpheus and Eurydice* (5ᵗʰ cent. B.C.); the statue of *Athena,* copy of an original of the school of Phidias; the *Doryphoros* from Pompeii, one of the finest copies of the original by Polycleitus; the *Ephebus,* also from Pompeii, copy of a 5ᵗʰ century B.C. original; the *Callipygian Venus,* after a Hellenistic original; the *Farnese Bull,* from Rome, copy of a Hellenistic original; the *Aphrodite Sosandra,* from Stabiae. The *Mosaics,* all from Pompeii, are in the mezzanine: the great *Battle of Darius and Alexander; marine fauna,* with a fight between an octopus and a lobster; *Roving Musicians; Plato's Academy; Scene of Magic.* On the upper floor are the finds from the *Villa of the Papyri* in Herculaneum, with stat-

ues and paintings. The ***Collection of Paintings*** includes: the portraits of *Paquius Proculus and his wife,* from Pompeii; many still lifes; *Di-*

▼ Pompeian mosaic
with a *Roving Musician*

ana Huntress and the so-called *Spring*, delicate paintings from Stabiae; *Knucklebone Players*, a monochrome from Herculaneum; *Theseus and the Minotaur*, from Pompeii; *Hercules and Telephos*, from Herculaneum. Of interest also the **Collection of Precious Objects**, the **Secret Cabinet** (special permission required) which contains erotic subjects, and the **Technology Section**, with tools and devices.

▲ Portrait of *Pasquius Proculus and his wife*, from Pompeii

▲ Fresco depicting *Spring*, from Pompeii

Palazzo Reale di Capodimonte

The monumentality, size and imposing architectural conception of this building, with pilasters vertically articulating the facade surmounted by a balustrade, justify its name as **Palace of Capodimonte**. Charles III of Bourbon commissioned it from Giovanni Antonio Medrano and Antonio Canevari (1738). This sovereign also founded the famous **royal porcelain manufactory**, active in

▼ Palazzo Reale di Capodimonte

▲ *Danaë*, by Titian

▼ *Flagellation*, by Caravaggio

the first half of the 18th century. It
was subsequently dismantled and
set up elsewhere, and eventually
closed in the early 19th century. All
around is the splendid Park (the
former **Woodlands of Capodimonte**), with breathtaking views
of the city framed by the gulf. The
initial installation of the first nucleus of works that now make up
the *Museum* and the *National Galleries of Capodimonte* was begun
by Charles of Bourbon, who had
first of all to see to the Farnese collections. Subsequent donations,
the acquisition of important private collections, as well as the need
to find a safe place for works in
some of the city's churches, made
this museum one of the most important in southern Italy, in particular for the internationally famous picture gallery. It contains

works by Tuscan, Umbrian, Venetian, Emilian, Lombard, foreign and – obviously – Neapolitan artists of varying periods and importance. A special section is devoted to 13th to 19th century Neapolitan artists, together with painters of other schools active in Naples. Among the most important, mention must be made of the *Crucifixion* (Masaccio), *Robert of Anjou Crowned by St. Louis of Toulouse* (Simone Martini), *Portrait of Francesco Gonzaga* (Mantegna), Portrait *of Paul III Farnese* (Titian), *Virgin and Child with angels* (Botticelli), *Madonna of the Assumption* (Masolino da Panicale), *Transfiguration* (Giovanni Bellini), *Flagellation* (Caravaggio), *Mystical Marriage of St. Catherine* (Correggio), *Sacra Conversazione* (Palma the Elder), *Madonna of Humility* (Roberto d'Oderisio), *Resurrection* (Sodoma), *Atalanta and Hippomenes* (Guido Reni), *The Blind Leading the Blind* (Pieter Brueghel), *Youth Lighting a Candle with a Coal* (El Greco), *Crucifix* (Antonis van Dyck). There are also precious objects, small bronzes, gold work, ivories and silverwork, including the *Farnese Coffer*. Particularly noteworthy in the **Royal Apartments**, with porcelains, various furnishings and fine furniture, is the *Porcelain Room* (second half 18th cent.). Decorative arts, works in porcelain and majolicas are the fulcrum of the **De Ciccio Collection**. In the **Tapestry Gallery** are fine pieces from the 16th century Belgian manufactory. One section is reserved for contemporary masters, with Alberto Burri, Mario Merz and Andy Warhol in the forefront.

▲ *Annunciation*, by Titian

▼ A room in the Palazzo Reale di Capodimonte

THE CITY UNDERGROUND

Catacombs of San Gennaro

Entrance to the catacombs is from the **Church of the Madre del Buon Consiglio**. One of the largest complexes in southern Italy, they are outstanding for the number of wall paintings, dating up to the 10th century. They date back to the 2nd century and are arranged on two subterranean levels. Of note among the frescoes is the one depicting *St. Gennaro*, of the 5th century, when the remains of the patron saint of the city were put there.

Catacombs of San Gaudioso

Entrance is from the Crypt of the **Church of S. Maria della Sanità**. This cemetery dates to the 5th century and contains the *Tomb of St. Gaudioso*. The mosaics and frescoes range from the 5th to the 6th centuries. In the 17th century portions of the catacombs were used in a rather unique way, for the cadavers were set to dry on hollow seats. When they were later walled up, the skulls were left visible, while the wall was decorated with subjects that commemorated the de-

ceased. The **Ossuary of the Fontanelle** is also located in the Sanità district. A considerable number of bones and skulls (the first skeletons date to after the plague of the 16th century) were placed in some of the tufa quarries and, in line with a curious folk custom, were cleaned and venerated by the families of the district. The **Catacombs of San Severo** with 5th century frescos are near the church of S. Severo.

A Walk underground

One of the entrances to the fascinating world of underground Naples is in the **Church of San Paolo Maggiore** where a portion of what is believed to have been the **Augustan Aqueduct** can be visited. Water was brought from Sarno to the wells in the city. The conduits were around 170 km long. The tour goes through a series of tunnels and cisterns of uncertain date and unspecified use. The custom of digging into the subsoil in the area, including the

excavation of building material, goes back to prehistory. The Greeks and Romans in turn kept up this custom, which continued throughout the centuries. In World War II the underground cavities served as air raid shelters. The effects of this millenary activity however have also been deleterious. Indeed, every so often a chasm opens up unexpectedly in the city streets. For an exciting experience, all one has to do is make advance reservations for a guided tour: "Napoli Sotterranea", Piazza San Gaetano, 68.

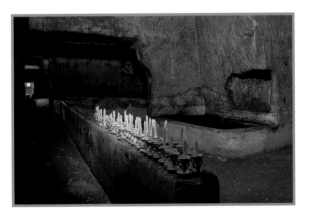

▲ Mt. Vesuvius during the last eruption in 1944 and the crater

Vesuvius

With its characteristic cone, Mount Vesuvius is one of the principal landmarks in the landscape around the Gulf of Naples. This active volcano, 1277 m. high, rises up from the old volcanic enclosure of **Mount Somma** (1132 m.). Historically Vesuvius first appeared on the scene in A.D. 79 when, a few years after an earthquake, it erupted and buried the neighboring cities under a sea of ashes and lapilli: Pompeii, Herculaneum, Stabiae. The Latin historian Pliny the Elder, who entered the disaster zone out of scientific curiosity, was both spectator and victim. His nephew, Pliny the Younger, at the time eighteen years old, reported the tragic events of the people who lived around Vesuvius. Eruptions have continued since then, the last in 1944. The area around Vesuvius has been famous since antiquity for its fertile lava soil, for its vineyards, which produce an excellent *Lachryma Christi*, and for the lovely 18th century villas in the towns around the volcano. An excursion to the crater is of great interest both for a sight of the spectacular cavity and for the marvelous panorama of Naples and the coast.

▲ The Sanctuary of the Madonna del Rosario in modern Pompeii

▲ Cast of a victim of the eruption, now in the Antiquarium

POMPEII

Pompeii was founded by the Osci, colonized by the Greeks in the 6ᵗʰ century B.C., and then conquered by the Samnites and the Romans. In A.D. 62 it was partially destroyed by an earthquake. In 79 the ashes of Vesuvius covered it completely and killed most of the inhabitants. As the ashes solidified, they encapsuled it in a crust several meters thick. For centuries the area was uninhabited. The first excavations began in the 18ᵗʰ century and became systematic in the 19ᵗʰ century. Today Pompeii is the best-preserved example of a Roman city and includes all types of buildings and pictorial decoration up to the first century A.D. This agricultural and trading city had warehouses, taverns, brothels, modest and patrician dwellings. The modern city, with its famous **Shrine of the Madonna del Rosario**, grew up near the archaeological area.

Porta Marina

This gate is set into the old Samnite walls of the city. It has two passageways, the one on the left for pedestrians, the other for vehicles.

▲ The Porta Marina, main entrance to the excavations

Remains of stables and warehouses are near the gate.

Antiquarium

The collection of antiquities includes finds from the excavations such as weapons, tools, sculpture, architectural fragments and pictorial decoration, vases and plaster casts of the shapes that the bodies of people and animals left in the solidified ashes. The more precious works of art found in Pompeii are in the Archaeological Museum in Naples.

▲▶ Men and animals were caught unawares by the eruption of Vesuvius

▲ Cast of a wheel in the Antiquarium

Basilica

The oldest public building in Pompeii where business and judicial affairs were carried out dates to the late 2nd century B.C. It had three aisles separated by 28 Corinthian columns and a podium at the back with two tiers of columns.

Forum

The center of public life in Pompeii, the forum consisted of a vast square surrounded by large buildings of political, religious and business nature. Entrance to the area was forbidden to wagons. In the Samnite and Roman period it was surrounded by a portico with powerful columns in tufa (the oldest) and travertine. Overlooking the Forum square are the **Basilica**, with one of its short sides; the **Temple**

▲ The Basilica from the colonnade of the "Tribunal"

of Apollo, erected by the Samnites and decorated with splendid statues, now replaced by copies; the **Temple of Jupiter**, at the center of the north side on a high podium, built in the 2nd century B.C. and dedicated to the *Capitoline triad* (Jupiter, Juno and Minerva); the

▼ View of the Forum

Macellum (covered market); the **Temple of Vespasian**, with a sculptured sacrificial altar; and the **Building of Eumachia**, built by the priestess Eumachia for the guild of weavers, with a lovely finely sculptured portal.

▲▼ The Temple of Apollo and the Temple of Vespasian

▲ The Temple of Jupiter

▲ The portico with marble columns, entrance to the Macellum

▼ The Building of Eumachia

Forum Baths

Well preserved, they date to the 1ˢᵗ century B.C. The various rooms are decorated with stuccowork. In the **tepidarium** there is a series of terracotta atlantes figures supporting a shelf. The heating system circulating hot air beneath the pavement is of note.

Villa of Mysteries

This magnificent suburban dwelling was built in the 2ⁿᵈ century B.C. and subsequently modified. After the earthquake of A.D. 62 the owners were transforming it into an agricultural estate when the eruption brought an end to the work and lives of its inhabitants. Some of the loveliest and most famous examples of Pompeian painting come from this villa. There was a spacious semicircular porticoed veranda overlooking the sea, where the present entrance is (the old entrance was on the opposite side). In the *tablinum* (meeting place, one of the principal rooms in the house) the walls are frescoed with Egyptian-style decorations on a black ground. On the right, after crossing a few rooms, is the **Hall of the Great Painting**, decorated with the famous frieze of the *Initiation into Dionysiac Mysteries*. This wall painting on red ground dates to the 1ˢᵗ century B.C. and is 17 meters long and 3 high. Various scenes show the initiation of a bride to the cult

▲ Tepidarium and calidarium in the Forum Baths

▼ Detail of the famous frieze that decorates the Hall of the Great Painting in the Villa of Mysteries

▲ *Dancing Satyr,*
fresco in the Villa of Mysteries

▼ The House of the Faun

▲ *Priapus,* god of fertility,
frescoed in the vestibule
of the House of the Vettii

of Dionysus. The phases include the reading of the ritual, the unveiling of the phallus (fertility symbol), flagellation by a winged female divinity and the dance.

House of the Faun

Imposing splendid example of the patrician *domus,* it probably belonged to a wealthy Roman statesman, but it dates back to the Samnite period (2nd century B.C.). The house has two atriums: the main one in Tuscan style, with a statuette of a *dancing Faun* (the original is in Naples) in the *impluvium,* and

the second, tetrastyle, for the passage of the service area. There are also two peristyles, the larger of which had two tiers of 44 columns each forming a portico around a large garden. Some of the finest mosaics in the Archaeological Museum in Naples, such as the famous *Battle of Darius and Alexander,* come from this house.

House of the Vettii

One of the richest and best pre-

served of Pompeian houses, it belonged to two wealthy merchants, Aulus Vettius Conviva and Aulus Vettius Restitutus. In addition to the fact that it represents a perfectly reconstructed Pompeian domestic interior, it is of particular note for its splendid paintings, dating to the last period of the city. A *Priapus* (god of fertility who appears, together with other phallic symbols, more or less everywhere in Pompeii as protection from the evil eye) is frescoed in the vestibule. There are two safes in the atrium. In a room to the left of the atrium we find frescoes of the *Sorrowing Cyparissus, Pan and Eros* and imaginary architectural structures. The atrium opens onto the peristyle with a garden, fountains that still have running water in them, statues and a Doric portico, with frescoed walls. Moving around the peristyle towards the right is a frescoed room, with *Daedalus and Pasiphae,* the *Myth of Ixios, Dionysus and Ariadne;* then comes the *Gynaeceum,* a complex of rooms

▼ *Sorrowing Cyparissus,*
fresco in the House of the Vettii

▲ Detail of the frieze with *cupids occupied in various activities* in the triclinium of the House of the Vettii

of which one near the kitchen is frescoed with erotic scenes. Lastly, in the great triclinium hall, magnificently decorated with paintings, of particular note is the frieze with *Cupids occupied in various activities* (goldsmiths, flower venders, harvesting grapes, involved in chariot races and in preparing perfumes), on black ground.

Stabian Baths

Imposing and extremely well preserved, they are the oldest in the city. They include a **Palaestra** (Gymnasium) with swimming pool and dressing rooms, **Men's Baths** and **Women's Baths**, with rooms covered with domes, elegant stucco decorations and niches for clothing.

Large Theater

It was built in the 2nd century B.C., exploiting the natural slope of the land. The **cavea**, divided into five sectors, could hold 5,000 spectators. Theater performances are still held there today.

Small Theater

Built in the 1st century B.C., it was an **odeion**, a small covered theater for mime and music. It seated about a thousand spectators.

▼ The Large Theater and the Small Theater

◄ The Stabian Baths

peii. Two shops connected with the interior opened on either side of the entrance. At the center of the atrium inside is the **impluvium**, or basin for collecting rainwater. The rooms leading off the atrium still have traces of their original decoration. Beyond is the peristyle with a hanging garden. From here to an upper pergola, with statues, fountains and a canal at the center. Still further on is the garden, with a long canal, once flanked by pergolas.

Amphitheater

Built in 80 B.C., this is the oldest extant Roman amphitheater. It had four orders of seats, the highest reserved for the women, and contained 20,000 spectators. A large awning, the **velarium**, shaded the spectators from the sun as they watched the gladiatorial games and wild animal hunts. In A.D. 59 a riot between Pompeians and Nucerians led to the prohibition of events in the amphitheater by the Roman Senate (the episode is depicted in a painting in the Archaeological Museum in Naples).

House of Loreius Tiburtinus

Spacious and elegant, with an imposing garden, this is one of the most interesting houses in Pom-

▲ The garden of the House of Loreius Tiburtinus and the canal that crosses it and one of the two frescoes on either side of the fountain, depicting *Pyramus and Thisbe*

▶ The Amphitheater

HERCULANEUM

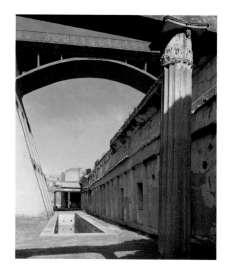

Founded by the Greeks (by Hercules according to an ancient legend), in 89 B.C. it became a Roman municipium. In 79 A.D. the eruption of Vesuvius buried it under an enormous flow of lava that solidified and preserved the houses. The first excavations date to the 18th century, but part of the city is still waiting to be dug out under the level of the modern town. Herculaneum is a typical Roman city of the 1st century A.D. The **Decumanus Maximus** or main street is intersected by the *cardini,* defining the rectangular *insulae* or city blocks, with baths and public buildings, villas and the theater not far from the city. In Insula IV is the **House of the Mosaic Atrium**, and the **House of the Wooden Par-** tition, which still has a carbonized wooden partition. The **Samnite House**, one of the oldest in the city, is on the right at the crossing with the Decumanus Inferiores. On the left are the **Baths**, a large complex divided into two sections, one for the men and one for the women, splendidly decorated. A bit further off, still on Cardo IV,

▼The floor with black and white squares that gave its name to the House of the Mosaic Atrium

▼The women's apodyterium of the Central Baths, with the splendid marble floor

▲View of Cardo III

▲▼ The relief with the *Myth of Telephos*, in the peristyle of the house of the same name and the garden of the House of the Gem

is the **House of Neptune and Amphitrite,** named after a mosaic in the nymphaeum depicting the two mythological figures. The **House of the Bicentennial** overlooks the Decumanus Maximus. Turning back on Cardo V on the left is the **Palaestra,** with a fine fountain. At the bottom of the cardo is the **House of the Relief of Telephos,** the **House of the Gem** and, opposite, the **House of the Deer,** with an elegant terrace overlooking the sea and two sculptural groups of *Deer attacked by dogs*. Nearby are the **Suburban Baths**.

▲ The Calidarium of the Suburban Baths

▲▶ The House of the Deer from the south and *Deer attacked by dogs*, one of the two sculptural groups that give the house its name

SORRENTO

Famous seaside resort on the gulf of Naples, Sorrento stands on a tufa bank rising sheer from the sea. It was already a favorite vacation site with the Romans. In the Middle Ages it was Byzantine, then an independent duchy and Nor-

man. Attacks by Saracen pirates were frequent. The poet Torquato Tasso was born here in 1544. The area abounds in citrus plantations, while silk and lace are some of the typical craft products. The **Cathedral** (considerably rebuilt in modern times) stands at the crossing of **Corso Italia** and **Via Tasso**, the main city streets. Of note inside are a *bishop's throne*,

▼ The enchanting Sorrentine coast

▲ Detail of the Moorish interlacing arches in the cloister of the Church of San Francesco

a *pulpit* dating to 16th century and a 15th century *Adoration of the Child*. The **Basilica of Sant'Antonino** is also of interest. It is medieval but was renovated in Baroque style. The *Tomb of the Saint* can be seen in the crypt, where an oratory existed as far back as the 14th century, later incorporated into the basilica. The interior, with a nave and two aisles, has numerous 17th century paintings and a fine **Nativity scene** or crèche in the sacristy, an example of 18th century folk art by the greatest Neapolitan sculptors of this genre. A visit to the *Sedile Dominova*, an elegant 15th century loggia, is also to be recommended, as well as to the **Church of San Francesco** and its charming *cloister* with Moorish interlaced arches dating to the 14th century. But above all go and see the *Museo Correale di Terranova*, installed in the 18th century palazzo of the counts of Terranova. The museum contains an extraordinary collection of minor arts (majolicas, Baroque Neapolitan furniture, Capodimonte porcelains and clocks) and paintings of Campanian school. Near Sorrento, at **Punta del Capo**, are the remains of the Roman **Villa of Pollius Felix**, rising up sheer over a tiny picturesque "cove" with tall rock cliffs on either side of the narrow passageway.

▼ Marina Grande and the Natural Arch rising sheer on the east coast of the island

CAPRI

Capri is one of the most famous Italian tourist resorts in the world, crowded in all seasons. The island rises up as a mass in a deep blue sea, with its splendid Mediterranean vegetation and deeply indented coastline, riddled with grot-

toes including the famous **Grotta Azzurra** or Blue Grotto, one of the loveliest in Italy. A small opening on the sea leads into a large space with an extraordinary blue light, where objects plunged into the water take on silvery tones. **Capri** is the island's main center, a charming picturesque town with low houses, winding streets, hotels and shops. It is particularly animated at New Year's with its famous popular festival. Other centers are **Marina Grande, Anacapri** and **Marina Piccola**. A small resort and bathing center on the southern coast, Marina Piccola is the point of departure for excursions by boat to the **Faraglioni**, enormous rocks rising up out of the clear sea.

▲▼The haunting interior of the Grotta Azzurra and the impressive Faraglioni

▼The famous piazzetta of Capri

ISCHIA

The wealth of mineral springs, fumaroles and spas on Ischia can be traced back to the volcanic origins of the island. The beauty of the landscape and the coast, together with the mild climate and the spas, attract a great number of tourists in all seasons. The fertile soil has favored the growth of splendid pine groves, citrus plantations and grapes. The Greeks who first colonized it in the 7th century B.C. called it *Pithecusa*. Then came the Neapolitans and Romans who made the most of it as a vacation resort.

▲ The picturesque marine hamlet
and a view of the islet with the Castle and the Convent of the Poor Claires

▲▼ The Aragonese Fortress, which furnishes a splendid view of Ischia

Subsequently it belonged to the Normans, the Angevin and the Aragonese and was frequently devastated and sacked by the Saracen pirates (which is why so many lookout towers were built).

Ischia is the most important center on the island, divided into two parts. **Ischia Porto** stretches out with its elegant streets, hotels and spas around the port, which is set in a volcanic crater. **Ischia Ponte** stands in the area of the **Aragonese Bridge**, built in 1438 to join the picturesque fisherman hamlet to the islet on which the **Aragonese fortress** and the former **Convent of the Poor Claires** stands.

▲▼Views of Amalfi

AMALFI

The Amalfi Coast is one of the most famous tourist areas in Italy. It includes the Sorrentine Peninsula from Sorrento to Salerno, and is one steep ravine after another, with stretches of coast falling sheer down to a deep blue sea, and with beaches and characteristic towns overlooking marvelous inlets. Amalfi is a stupendous tourist town, one of the most popular in Italy thanks to its beauty and art. Founded by the Romans, it reached its maximum splendor in the Middle Ages. As a free Republic (the oldest of the Italian Maritime Republics), it long dominated commerce in the Mediterranean with its fleet, contributing to the history of navigation with the first maritime code, the *Tavole Amalfitane*, and perfecting the compass (by Flavio Gioia). Defeated and sacked by Pisa, it began to decline in the 12th century. Every year a crew takes part in the historic **Regatta of the Maritime Republics**. The principal monument in the city is the **Cathedral**, founded prior

to the 9th century and remodeled more than once. It stands in a scenic position on a tall flight of steps. The facade with its varied forms and two-colored stone is a 19th century renovation in Gothic style. The upper part of the bell tower (12th-13th century) is in Moorish style, with majolica revetment. An extraordinary *bronze door* on the main entrance was made in Constantinople around the middle of the 11th century. Inside the church are two *Romanesque pulpits*, an ancient *baptismal font* and, in the crypt, the remains of the apostle Saint Andrew. From the Cathedral access is to the delightful **Chiostro del Paradiso**, built in 1268 in Moorish style with pointed interlacing arches. Interesting archaeological finds are on exhibit under the portico.

▶ The splendid Cathedral of Amalfi

PAESTUM

Paestum is one of the most important archaeological sites in Italy. It was founded by Greek colonists in the 7th century B.C. and was named *Poseidonia*, or city of Poseidon. By the time the Lucanians conquered the town at the end of the 5th century BC. and changed the name to *Paistom*, it had already achieved a prominent position throughout the plain of the Sele river. In 273 B.C. it became a Roman colony, one of the most flourishing and faithful in the Latin world. Its fortunes waned in the early Middle Ages, when the harbor was silted over and malaria became rife. In the 9th century Saracen raids convinced the last few inhabitants to abandon the site. Paes-

▼ The Basilica, the oldest of the temples in Paestum

▲ A view of the Basilica

▼ The Temple of Ceres

tum was overrun by vegetation and forgotten until the 18th century and the most recent excavations. It now offers visitors a vast archaeological area with streets, the remains of dwellings, theaters, baths and splendid Doric temples. Archaeological finds are on exhibit in the Museum. The **Temple of Ceres**, actually dedicated to Athena, was built at the end of the 6th century B.C. There are thirteen columns on the long sides and six on the front and back where the pediments and architraves are also still in existence. The cell inside is preceded by a *pronaos* of which the column bases are still extant. In the Middle Ages the temple was transformed into a Christian church. The **Temple of Neptune**, built around the middle of the 5th century B.C. and dedicated to the Argive Hera, is among the most beautiful and best examples of Doric architecture. It is of imposing size and elegance: the columns, with their accentuated entasis or curve, have a warm golden hue, spellbinding at sunset. The **Basilica** is the oldest temple, dating to the middle of the 6th century B.C. and was dedicated to Hera. It still has its entire portico of fifty columns.